Dear reader,

If you have ever dreamed of writing, publishing, and sharing your book with thousands of people, then *Becoming a Bestselling Author* by prolific Christian author, Dr. Larry Keefauver, is the perfect book for you. Not only does it provide valuable insight on writing and publishing your book, but also on reaching and impacting scores of people with your life-changing message.

As Director of Acquisitions for Xulon Press, it gives me great pleasure to announce that Dr. Keefauver's book is one of our highest recommended books for 2017. *Becoming a Bestselling Author* has received our distinguished Editor's Choice commendation as a must read for all aspiring Christian authors, speakers, teachers, business professionals and church leaders.

I have personally worked with Dr. Keefauver in ministry, publishing, and business for nearly two decades. He shares directly from the heart, and the Lord. His stories are sure to encourage, equip, and empower you to develop a business plan for marketing and selling your book. Imagine thousands of people buying and reading your book!

So, settle in with this top read and discover the many ways God will use you, and your book, to impact the lives of many. Let's get to work, and write to expand the Kingdom of God.

Donald Newman
Director of Acquisitions
Xulon Press Publishing Company

EDITOR'S CHOICE

ENDORSEMENTS

Thanks to this quick and easy read, Christian authors can find practical helps for spreading their message. I especially enjoyed the personal stories that showed these tips aren't theoretical--they really work. The proven pointers are real examples of the hard work and dedication it takes to partner with God to get published.

-Joani Schultz, Chief Creative Officer, Group Publishing

A good portion of those in ministry and market place would love to write a great book, but simply do not know where to begin. In his latest book, "Becoming a Bestselling Author: 21 Proven, Profitable Pointers for Marketing and Selling You & Your Message," bestselling author, Dr. Larry Keefauver provides just such a roadmap to achieve that dream for authors, both novice and professional. Who better to address the issues of writing a book from cover-to-cover than Larry Keefauver, having written 15 bestselling books? I highly recommend this outstanding book for those who have yet to pen their soul, thoughts and dreams with ink and parchment, or write again, even more professionally.

-Marcus D. Lamb, Founder – President, Daystar Television Network

----

Larry Keefauver knows what he's writing about. Who better to coach authors on how to become a bestselling author than someone who has authored sixty-plus books, edited, ghostwritten and mentored dozens of published writers? Dr. Larry provides practical, proven and doable pointers for marketing and selling who you are, and the message inside you that must be shared.

-**Dr. Jimmy Knott** , Teaching Pastor, First Baptist Orlando, FL

When it comes to the craft of writing, publishing, and marketing a book, Larry Keefauver is the master craftsman. In his latest book, Larry generously shares with us a wealth of "trade secrets" acquired and honed over a lifetime of producing successful books. By reading "Becoming a Bestselling Author," you and I can know the same deep and joyful satisfaction Larry has experienced in seeing a story, a message, or a lesson committed to print and preserved for the ages. I've personally benefited from Larry's professional coaching, and I will always be grateful to God and to him for it. Bravo, Larry! This is one of your best works—which is saying a lot—and one of the greatest gifts you could ever give to the rest of us! Thank God and thank you!

-**Dr. Rob Schneck**, President and Lead Missionary of Faith and Action, Washington, D.C.

Two things always happen when I speak with Dr. Keefauver or read one of his books: I am lifted up and humbled. I am lifted up because Dr.

Larry is always grounded in the essence of writing and publishing, that being the message of Christ as Lord and Savior. When I stay focused on Christ all things are possible and I am uplifted. My ego then is forced to find humility and I know I was caught in the importance of "me" not the message of Christ. "Becoming a Bestselling Author" will uplift you and humble you and lead you to the joy and success of having YOUR book published and PURCHASED by the very person God has waiting. Our book, "5 Minutes at a Time," is further proof of the love, compassion and talent of Dr. Larry and I hope the clear example of the message of Christ and our humility.

-**Kris Hager**, Gold Star Dad, Salem Communications Radio Host of "5 Minutes at a Time." Parrish, FL

Dr. Larry Keefauver has been a prolific author, senior editor of a major magazine, and involved in the book selling industry for several decades. I have found him to be extremely knowledgeable and experienced in all aspects of this field. I highly recommend this book for both new and experienced writers.

-**Dr Joseph Mattera**, Convener of the United States Coalition of Apostolic Leaders

----

I am honored to endorse "Becoming a Bestselling Author" by Dr Larry Keefauver. This book is not only an excellent resource for those desiring to write but also a great read for all leaders. This book will give you practical and relevant principles for writing and leading in the Church and

marketplace. I have read and promoted many of his books over the last fifteen years. Dr Larry is an outstanding author, teacher, and friend.

-**Dr. Ronald V. Burgio**, Lead Pastor, Love Joy Church – www.lovejoy. org "Reaching People, Developing Leaders, Making a Difference" and President Emeritus, Elim Fellowship –www.elimfellowship.org "To strengthen the leader, to equip the church, to reach the world"

"Becoming a Bestselling Author" is a must-have reference book for every writer. Dr. Larry skillfully maps on how to market and sell your book before it's completed. Dr. Larry was so instrumental in helping me with my book project. I know that you will be blessed and enlightened with the wisdom that you will gain from this treasure.

-**Dana Rosser**, Author of *"Thru Thick & Thin"*

My friend, Dr. Larry Keefauver, has written an amazing new book, "Becoming a Bestselling Author," for both aspiring writers and experienced authors. This book is filled with practical insights including how to get started, the actual writing experience, how to build a writing team, and gives critical insights into marketing your ideas. "Becoming a Bestselling Author" is a must-read and will be a great help to you. I highly recommend this book to you!

-**Larry Kreider**, International Director of DOVE International, Author of forty books

----

The pointers listed in "Becoming a Bestselling Author" have equipped me to spread the message of my book in a more powerful way for God's glory. Thanks Dr. Larry!"

-Dawn D. Mitchell, Author of *"Light After a Layoff: Seven Spiritual Keys to Strengthen Resilience in the Midst of a Job Loss, Career Transition, or Professional Setback"*

Any person desiring to become a best-selling author must read Dr. Larry Keefauver's "Becoming a Bestselling Author." This book is full of ideas and information from a bestselling author that would benefit any author. Dr. Keefauver has a fascinating track record in the book writing and producing world and this record can ignite hope in every author, to not just write a book, but write a bestselling one. I highly recommend this book filled with how-to's from beginning to end of the writing journey.

-Dr. Jim Buckley, co-author of *Walking Across America: One Step at a Time* (with Dr. Larry Keefauver, senior editor)

My husband, Jim, and I first came to know Dr. Larry Keefauver when he became our editor for our own book about Jim's walk across America. I have found Dr. Keefauver's latest book, "Becoming a Bestselling Author," to be full of helpful insight with clear, practical steps to follow. Not only does he tell how to become a bestselling author, he inspires through real-life stories from his own life and the lives of others.

-Glenda Buckley, Co-author of *"Walking Across America: One Step at a Time"* www.invitingAmericahome.org

Whether your passion is to deliver a message or jumpstart a writing career you need this book. All the creative devotion and discipline to write a compelling book does not get it into the hands of those who need to read it. "BECOMING A BESTSELLING AUTHOR" provides time-tested, market-proven, and spirit-inspired strategies to do just that: launch your book and propel your career. It did for me."

-**Robert F Lane M.D.**, Medical Oncologist, author Cancer's Bell Lap and The Dragon Behind the Door (2016), Cancer's Windrunners (2017). Founding Director Northwest Cancer Center, Northwest Hospice

Dr. Larry Keefauver has "cracked the code" and shared it with us all in his latest book, "Becoming a Bestselling Author." I can't think of a more straightforward, user-friendly map for Christian authors to share the vision that God has placed upon their heart. Do not place the "cart before the horse!" Read this book and follow its instructions before you contact an editor, publisher, or sign a contract. In fact, if I "called the shots" in Christian self-publishing, I would build this book into all my publishing contracts and require aspiring authors to compose a draft of answers to the question, "What do you need to strategize for or implement?" at the end of each chapter. I know this sounds absurd but I cannot emphasize how essential this book is to anyone seeking to impact the Kingdom of God through publishing his or her God-given story.

-**Commander David Reid Brown**, Chaplain Corps, U.S. Navy (Ret.)

Are you a first time publisher/author? Larry's book is a must read! Larry is an excellent editor and writing consultant. As a bestselling author and award-winning sales executive, Larry helped me compose my latest book, *"Instinctology, A Leadership Method for Turning GUT Instincts into Concrete Action."* Thank you, Larry, for your guidance and wisdom!

-**Roben Graziadei**, M.A., Chief Instinctology Officer, Founder/ Speaker/Best Selling Author of *"Instinctology, A Leadership Method for Turning GUT Instincts into Concrete Action!"*

I had the urge to write a business book for many years. I never got serious about it because I had no idea how to bring my thoughts, stories and ideas, that I had accumulated over 40 years, into an organized thoughtful manuscript. I heard about Dr. Larry from my associate and decided to call him and discuss the possibility of Dr. Larry ghostwriting my book. After discussing the overall concept of a business book with Dr. Larry, he convinced me that I should do the writing with his coaching and assistance. The concepts and practical information that Dr. Larry speaks of in his new book "Becoming a Bestselling Author" is the process that he used in helping me get my manuscript written and published. I would highly recommend to anyone that wants to write a book about any subject, from Business to Fiction, read and utilize the concepts spelled out in Dr. Larry's book.

-**Karl Eberle**, a veteran of the manufacturing industry with proven results in delivering profitable, efficient leadership strategies. He was a senior VP of Manufacturing at Harley Davidson and a division manager at John Deere. For the past five years, Karl has worked as a trusted multi-industry consultant, helping improve their effectiveness. He is co-author of *"Profit Through Change."*

I have lived through the advice that Dr. Larry Keefauver gives in "Becoming a Bestselling Author." Larry has been the editor of the first two books I have written, and I look forward to working with him on my third. I have never written before, and his advice was invaluable. With his extensive experience and maturity as a pastor, Christian writer, editor, counselor and speaker, he brings in his books and in his editorial advice, truth, wisdom, and encouragement. Many times, I have floundered, been short on hope and questioned my goals, only to have him pick me up and gently point me in the right direction. God has blessed me in having found him. I whole-heartedly recommend his most recent book. It is biblically sound, technically helpful and filled with good advice that is uplifting and focused. He knows whereof he speaks.

-**Irving S. Wiesner**, M.D. Psychiatrist and author of Tools from Psychiatry for the Journey of Faith, Christian Identity; Sexuality and Relationships: A Psychiatrist Answers Your Questions, and the upcoming, Health and Sickness in Today's Church: A Psychiatrist Offers a Prescription for Healing and Growth

---

Dr. Larry Keefauver is an accomplished author/coach who helped me finish an autobiographical book called "A Reason to Hope." It is quite a task to write a book. Marketing and developing a successful business plan that will get your book into the hands of your target audience can be a greater challenge. In his book, "Becoming a Bestselling Author," Dr. Keefauver identified proven strategies and coaching tips that were needed to take my book to the next level. I read how multiple books with diverse themes were distributed into the hands of his target audience. Why reinvent the wheel? Dr. Keefauver is a bestselling author and also a proven coach/motivator. I highly recommend that you read his book as well.

-Jeffrey Siegel, President Global Youth Baseball Federation, Inc.

Dr. Larry Keefauver was our technical editor for the book I co-authored with Karl Eberle. Our book, "Profit for Change" was a journey of learning. The journey in itself is sometimes quite difficult but Larry was our calm in the storm. He guides the reader to understand the purpose of the book, and uses his life experiences in creating successful books. The purpose of our book was to tell a story that the reader could experience. He announced to us in the summer of 2016, that his new book, "Becoming a Bestselling Author," would mirror much of our journey with him in creating our book. As I read through his manuscript, I found that it was well written and reads in an interesting manner that makes a reader want to turn to the next page, and read more. Through the steps outlined in his book, Larry coached us in developing our book for the business market, and we grew professionally from his editing, training, and coaching. This book will become a must read. His story needs to be published and read by authors from all backgrounds.

-**Manny Barriger**, CEO Rent-A-Blackbelt®, co-author of *"Profit Through Change"*

BECOMING A
BESTSELLING AUTHOR

21 Proven, Profitable Pointers for Marketing and Selling You & Your Message

DR. LARRY KEEFAUVER

www.xulonpress.com

DEDICATION

Dedicated to God the Father, Jesus Christ the Son,
and the Holy Spirit.

Also dedicated to my wife, Judi, who has so believed in me as
we celebrate over forty-seven years in marriage at this book's
publication, and the joy of parenting, ministering
and writing together.

Dedicated also to our children, their spouses, our seven
grandchildren, their future spouses, and all generations to come.
May the Lord Jesus Christ have mercy on them, and all generations
to come in the name of the
Father, Son, and Holy Spirit.
Amen.

Finally, I dedicate this book to my dear friend, J. David Stone, who
made me write and publish my first material with Abingdon Press
and co-authored with me our first bestselling book.
Love you eternally, my friend in Christ.

ACKNOWLEDGMENTS

Special thanks to all the publishers and editors who over the past four decades have encouraged, equipped, educated, and supported me in my many writing, editing, and publishing projects.

While I am in danger of missing some very important friends and colleagues to whom I apologize in advance, I want to thank in particular Mike Hyatt at Thomas Nelson, Rolf Zetterson at Hachette, Steve Strang and Tom Freiling at Charisma, the late Guy Morrell and his family at Bridge Logos, Thom and Joani Schultz at Group, the wonderful staffs at Gospel Light, the wonderful staff and editors at the American Bible Society, David C. Cook Publishing, and Lifeway, Philis Boulinghouse at Howard/Simon and Schuster, my literary agent, Lois de la Haba, and Chad Nycamp and Don Newman at Xulon Press, Raymond Mooi and Li Ming at Acts Global Network and their entire staff, and Gary Haynes my dear friend and publisher at Atos in Brazil. Finally, to Robert Stearns and all the dear friends at Eagles Wings particularly Veronica and Stephen Jenks who have been so encouraging and supportive of my writing and ministry.

Thank you to Tony Tseng, Winifred Yeh, and all the wonderful staff at GoodTV in Taipei, Taiwan, who broadcast our 200+ Family Forum programs and published so many of my books in Mandarin.

I so appreciate the input given to me on this book in terms of content and editing by Mark Norris, Pam McLaughlin, Jim and Glenda Buckley, Dr. Dennis Golden, Roben Graziadei, Christy Osborn, Pierre Eade, Don Newman, David Youngren, Wayne Mendoza, and scores of other friends and colleagues.

This book and my writing of it would not be possible without the encouragement and friendship of Dave and Janie Hail, Dr. Buddy Crum, the staff at Xulon, Kris Hager at Salem Communication, as well as Jack and Pam McLaughlin, Dr. Keith Johnson, Dr. Ron Burgio, Dr. Ron Cottle, Sam Hinn, Marcus and Joni Lamb, and Pastor Bob and Nancy Engelhardt.

The Board of YMCS including Dr. Tom Gill, the McLaughlins, Peter Keefauver, Judi Keefauver, Al and Julie Roe, and the support over the years of writing and missions travel given by our wonderful prayer and support partners particularly Red and Dee Tiner, Pat and Liz Keefauver, Lee and Amy Bozeman, Peter and Loren Keefauver, Al and Kim Keefauver, Tom and Cathy Laws, First Christian Church of Ft. Lauderdale, Fl, and so many others through the years too numerous to name but certainly praiseworthy…How I thank the Lord for them all.

Knowing I have missed so many, I still want to thank the Lord for the churches and Christians around the world that have read and given input to me for my books. Also, much gratitude goes to all the hundreds of Christian leaders in the church and in business who have given me the privilege of editing and ghostwriting for them. Wow, what a ride and learning experience for me in my writing and publishing.

TABLE OF CONTENTS

FOREWORD

by Bishop Robert Stearns & Dr. Tommy Reid

I have had the great privilege of knowing Dr. Larry Keefauver as a friend, mentor, counselor, consultant, and pastor for close to 20 years. I have been with him on dozens of occasions in dozens of different settings and contexts. His gift is the gift of communication. He has an extraordinary ability to teach you and model for you the ways for your message not only to have depth, but also to be heard broadly.

I am tremendously excited about his new book – "Becoming a Bestselling Author." Dr. Larry has been involved in some capacity in every one of the five books I have written. All my books are still in print, many have been translated into languages around the world, and I am humbled that the thoughts that I believe the Lord inspired in me are impacting so many others. That is, in a not insignificant degree, attributable to the capable skills of Dr. Larry. He has shaped and guided me as a communicator, and I am forever grateful.

Whatever type of writing you are doing, whatever ways you are communicating, you will learn and grow from this book. Its lessons will be signposts along your communication highway, safely leading you to a destination called IMPACT.

Happy Communicating!

-**Bishop Robert Stearns**, Founder and Executive Director of Eagles Wings, Bishop of The Tabernacle, Buffalo, New York

----

Over the years I have had the privilege of authoring eight books. My first, "The Exploding Church," became a bestseller overnight. Others, which still think are more significant, sold very few. I learned by default much of what my friend, Larry Keefauver, shares in his new book from my own "School of Hard Knocks." I wish someone had written this book before I wrote mine. I would not have needed to suffer in that school. But no one had written this book before I wrote mine. I know if I had read this one, I would have multiplied the number of people who would have been inspired by my writing.

For today's "want to be author" that significant book is now available. It asks all of the questions that I wish I would have asked. It answers all of the questions that I should have researched before I wrote my first book. It is informative but at the same time inspirational. It is factual and realistic, but at the same time it does not crush a dream but beings life to a dream. If you are truly a person who has a dream of writing a book, "Becoming a Best Selling Author," is MUST for you.

Larry Keefauver has an ability to inspire the reader, and this book is truly inspirational. Larry has an ability to "tell it all" and he does, but never with the intent or the result of trying to make a huge task seem impossible, but rather to inspire you to dot all the "i's" and cross all the "t's", because if you do not do so, you will not succeed. This is truly the guide book on succeeding or to be more specific to make succeeding simple.

Most of this book comes from the pen of one of the most successful authors in the world today. He succeeded not only in writing great manuscripts, but in writing them so people would gain knowledge and be inspired. And this author marketed what he wrote. He not only tells you how to write a book, but how to market a book. Your success as a writer would not be a success if you wrote the greatest book in the world but no one bought it. So write... but as Larry inspires us... sell what you write.

So, if you have a dream to write a book... this is for you... read this, put your dream on paper and inspire the world to read it!

-**Dr. Tommy Reid**, Colden, New York, Bishop Emeritus, The Tabernacle

INTRODUCTION

Taking Your Message to Market and Your Books to Branding

Almost weekly, a few authors call me asking something like, "Dr. Larry, can you help me market and sell my books? I have ten cases of books in storage and don't know how to promote and publicize them." In talking with them, I usually discover they didn't know at the beginning of their book writing and publishing venture, that they didn't have a business plan for writing, editing, producing, printing, publishing, distributing, marketing, and selling their book.

Unfortunately, it's almost impossible to implement a successful marketing and sales plan after the fact. So, the purpose of this book is very specific and simple. Every book project and all publishing ventures need a business plan that identifies the people, processes, products involved with timelines, costs, goals, and objectives. That business plan includes the marketing and sales strategies needed to put the published material in the hands of as many readers, listeners, viewers, and followers as possible.

Over the past forty years, I have pastored, taught, written, and published over sixty books and curriculum series with fifteen best-sellers, over two million in sales, and published in twelve languages. I have edited and ghostwritten for hundreds of published authors, many of whom have become bestselling Christian authors. I have also coached scores of authors from beginning to end in taking their books to branding themselves as speakers, consultants, business leaders, teachers, coaches, and leaders in many areas of culture, business, church, finance, health and wellness, medicine, psychology and psychiatry, education, media, and government.

My education as a pastoral psychologist and experience in business, ministry, publishing, writing, editing, and marketing has equipped me to coach and help authors from many backgrounds with messages coming in many forms—fiction, non-fiction, poetry, screen-plays, dissertations, textbooks, curriculum, memoirs, audios, online courses, and webinars, etc. In writing this book, I am sharing with you what I have learned in becoming a bestselling author. I will practically explain to you the *21 Proven, Profitable Pointers for Marketing and Selling You & Your Message.*

Without further delay, join me on the journey to becoming a bestselling author!

Read on!

-1-

Sow What's in Your Bag

The first time my good friend and publisher, Dave Hail, said to me, "Sow what's in your bag," I knew this was the point at which writing bestselling books starts. What comes immediately to mind is Jesus—His words, stories, parables, similes, teachings, and discipling others. He sowed what was in His bag.

"Listen! Behold, a sower went out to sow...."[1] Jesus' parable about a sower illustrates this first pointer for becoming a bestselling Christian author. Authors sow the words, stories, dreams, visions, experiences and memories, studies, thoughts, feelings, hope, faith, and love that's in their bags. In addition to a sower (the author), two items are essential for sowing—seed and a bag. Books begin with words, the seeds, which grow into thoughts, phrases, sentences, paragraphs, anecdotes, illustrations, teachings, messages, pericopes, chapters, sections, books, etc.

Words. You don't need a Harvard vocabulary to write or speak, but you need words particularly suited to listeners and readers with whom you must communicate. My grandparents and parents hooked me on playing Scrabble° at a young age. In those days without video games, board games like Parcheesi, Checkers, Chess, Monopoly°, Risk°, card games, and the like were king of my free time. To entertain myself, I would organize fantasy tournaments and play Scrabble° for hours, days, and even weeks on end. Of course, I had a dictionary at hand and would look up words, read definitions, practice using them in sentences, and put together endless combinations on the board.

Over the years as I spoke and wrote, the power of words impacted and empowered me to become an author. My ongoing prayer has been, "Let the words of my mouth and the meditation of my heart be acceptable in thy sight, O Lord, my strength, and my redeemer."[2]

Stories. Stories fascinated me. I loved to read books, especially biographies. The most impactful biography for me was *A Man Called Peter*, written by his wife, Catherine Marshall. His remarkable journey to become first a preacher and then Chaplain of the Senate inspired me. Most life-changing for me were Bible stories creatively written for young readers by Elsie Egermeier, *Egermeier's Bible Story Book*. I loved the pictures and read it from cover to cover dozens of times in my elementary years. This laid the foundation for me to read, study, and love the Scriptures.

By speaking and writing books, telling stories, including anecdotal material, providing illustrations, and painting word pictures, I learned much about communicating to listeners and readers' life-changing and impactful ideas, concepts, and truths. I started collecting stories by memory and writing them down from magazines, newspapers, sermons, teachers, politicians, and other writers.

> **By whatever means you can, collect and remember stories;
> they are the salt and pepper of speaking and writing.**

Dreams and Visions. One night after reading Egermeier's retelling of Isaiah's vision (Isaiah 6), I fell asleep replaying that fiery scene over and over again on the screen of my mind. In the middle of the night, I was awakened startled by a thunderous boom with almost blinding light filling my room. My body tingled with fiery shock and awe. A voice spoke to me about speaking God's words to the world. I asked for His hot coals to touch my tongue like he had done for Isaiah. In that moment, the ancient prophet's vision was etched eternally in my mind; his visionary calling became mine. As he had become a preacher and writer, so I desired to take God's good news to the world. Decades later, Judi and I would have the privilege of traveling to Eastern Europe, Brazil, Canada, India, Southeast Asia, and throughout the U.S. taking books, teachings, and recordings (radio and television) to others.

Bestselling books often start with a dream, vision, or even a nightmare. The bestselling *Lord I Wish* series' book, *Lord I Wish My Family Would Get Saved*, started with a dream, or rather a nightmare when I saw my brother at God's judgment among the goats. I awoke trembling in fear, drenched with sweat. Taking a shower at 3:00 a.m., I wept and cried out to God, "Why isn't my brother saved?"

"You are the reason," the Spirit whispered. For the next week, the Spirit convicted me of the sinful walls I had built between myself, my brother, and even God—walls of spiritual arrogance, a critical spirit, faithlessness, and prayerlessness. That book poured out of me and reached tens of thousands in English, Chinese, and Portuguese. Through their agreement in prayer with me in reading the book, not only were scores of family members saved, my brother was also wonderfully redeemed.

God may have used a dream, vision, or even a word spoken through someone else to convict you to write the vision down:

> *Write the vision*
> *And make it plain on tablets,*
> *That he may run who reads it.*
> (Habakkuk 2:2)

Throughout the Scriptures, we are commanded to both "hear and obey." Stop procrastinating. Just do it. Write your book.

Experiences and memories. Knowing that God works for good in all things for all those who love Him and are called according to His purposes, we can be assured that virtually any and even all of our experiences in life can be used for His good. Many of our life experiences can be used in our books. I often tell authors whom I coach, edit, or ghostwrite for that it's not enough just to write down your life story as a testimony or witness. More is required than simply telling a story—it needs to be unpacked in such a way that the reader can learn what God was doing in and through you and your situation.

When experiences are shared, they need to be I³. The **first** "I" in I³ is *Instruction & Information*. Many authors get so caught up in ["facts" (as important and truthful as they can be) that they're all they give the reader. Such a book might well be like a textbook, but could lack the other two needed ingredients to bake the cake.

The **second** "I" in I³ is *Inspiration & Impartation*. When the New Testament reveals that "all scripture is inspired," a literal translation of that Greek word is "God-breathed." Let God's Spirit breathe through your experiences. One Old Testament scholar spoke about reading the biblical narratives emphasizing that "God is the hidden actor" behind every story. Allow your experiences to become a window for the reader to see not just your *history* but *His-story* working in, through, around, and in spite of you. The good, the bad, and the ugly of your life can become the inspired instrument through which God's Spirit imparts His truth and Christ incarnated Himself to the reader. When your story is imparted to the reader, it becomes an icon or example of how God can love, forgive, change, and transform them into the image of Christ: "But we all, with unveiled face, beholding as in a mirror the glory of the Lord, are being transformed into the same image from glory to glory, just as by the Spirit of the Lord."[3]

The **third** "I" in I³ is *Implementation & Impact*. Be it fiction or non-fiction, biography or autobiography, testimony or teaching, poetry or prose, or any other type or genre, your book can impact (forcefully change or move) readers. God can use your book to deliver a word from Him to heal, save, or deliver. The truths, principles, and wisdom God speaks through your words can give readers true thoughts to think, positive feelings to feel, and right actions to implement in repentance, restoration, renewal, or to restart a relationship with themselves, others, or God. Powerful!

Often an author shares with me an idea or a whole manuscript for a book and asks me,

"Is my book worthwhile?"

Any God-mandated message if only read by one person who is instructed, informed, inspired, imparted to, and impacted is worth being written and published.

I was coaching and ghostwriting with a first-time writer/author living in London. He had immigrated from Africa and married a woman from his native village to bring with him. A few years into his new marriage and new life in the British Isles, he discovered that she had only married him to get out of Africa and that she was pregnant to boot! Her plan was to get to a new country, have a child from the union, and to start a new family without him!

Following a long, devastating divorce and custody battle filled with acrimony and abuse from both parties, the court awarded a foster family custody of their child. Each parent could only contact their daughter once a year with a gift and card on her birthday. No visits, phone calls, or any other form of contact was permitted until she was eighteen.

After that judge's ruling, God spoke to the father telling him to write a book about his life with all its trials, tests, and hardships. He connected with me through Xulon Press, told me his story through Skype, and I helped him write the book. After almost a year of hard work and tears, the book was finished. He had hoped to have a published book to take with him to churches throughout the UK and America, sharing his testimony about what God did in him to transform his hurt and anger into healing and forgiveness.

As we prepared his manuscript for production and publication, this Christian father told me through heart-wrenching sobs, "I can't do this. I cannot take this book to scores of churches and reveal my story. It could hurt my ex-wife. I can't do that. I will never publish this."

"Who did you write this book for?" I asked. The long interviews and talks he and I had journeyed through had brought us into a trusting friendship. I knew he would be honest with me.

After a few moments, he pensively lamented, "I thought I was writing a bestselling book that could open the door for me to preach and teach in churches. I discovered that the only person who really cares about or would read this story is me. Yes, I wrote it for me. It has helped me learn to forgive, hear God, and heal."

"You wrote it only for yourself?"

"Yes, I will never publish it," he replied.

"What about your daughter?"

First there was silence, then a sob, then some five minutes (seemed like an eternity) of anguished weeping erupted from the author's gut. Finally, the emotional storm subsided. Quietly he whispered, "Yes, I will publish only a handful of this book. Someday, I will be able to sign and give my book to her. She will learn the truth and know how much I love her...and God, her real father, loves her." Written for an audience of one, an eighteen-year old daughter in a few years will read a life-changing book written out of a father's obedience to the Father to "write the book."

Studies. You may laugh at me, but every single college, seminary, and post-graduate course I had taken along with my notes and papers, I have saved. Recently, my wife scanned all of them into computer files. My notes from sermon preparation including my slides, overheads, and power points have been digitally saved. Important books, journals, and articles along with my notes on them have been saved. I cannot remember everything I studied over the years, but the important stuff is all there. That information wasn't gleaned just to learn for the moment and pass exams. I was collecting seed. My journals from mission trips and prayer/devotional times have been wonderful "prime the pump" sources for my writing and publishing over sixty books and curriculum courses in twelve languages with an estimated sales and distribution of over two million worldwide. I tell you this out of amazement. I simply have been sowing what's in my bag, working hard at the cultivation of a writing skill, talent, and gift, and learning that God gave the increase.

What seed is in your bag?

Thoughts and Feelings. In writing my bestselling books, I have learned to be truthful (transparent) and candid—sharing the good, bad, and ugly about myself. Repentance and confession are good for the soul. In a way, much of writing is cathartic. As a pastoral psychologist, with Christ as my garbage man and therapist, I have learned in my writing that I am as Henri Nouwen calls us pastoral types—a wounded healer.

When authors share the honest thoughts and positive or negative emotions in their bags, they build a trusting rapport with their readers. An author's candid sharing helps the reader not only identify with the author, but also come to understand how God could work in and through them just as the Father did in the author's soul. What's real for the author on the inside can become real to the reader. As I am writing you, just as I wrote my bestselling books, I started the only place any author can start—from the inside out. Even when writing about others, I cannot begin to know how they felt or thought, but only report what they said and did through the filter of my own soul's mindset. Such sharing connects the author and reader just as if they were sitting down across from one another having intimate discourse—a three-way conversation among God, the author, and the reader.

I read a book by renown Duke basketball coach, Mike Krzyzwski, entitled *Leading with the Heart*. He wrote about getting organized, building a team, establishing discipline, and being dynamic. Much of what he wrote can be applied to *Writing from the Heart*. Such writing begins with truthfully sharing of your own thoughts and feelings. Remember that a book isn't a research document or a dissertation. A bestselling book begins with truthful thoughts and honest feelings. Readers aren't interested in what everyone has said about your subject; they hunger and thirst for creativity, originality, and freshness just as our body craves fresh food and clean water. My paraphrase of a familiar proverb, *As a man thinketh in his heart, so is he*[4], might be: *As a writer shares honest thoughts and feelings in a book, so the book reveals who the author really is.* **Write from the heart.**

Faith, hope, and love. Perhaps you haven't thought about these seeds—faith, hope, and love—being in your bag. Nonetheless, they need to be if your book will have life-changing impact on your readers. Later in this book I talk about "write to the market." I have learned that my bestselling books have usually answered questions or meet needs of my market profile readers. More about how you write to market later. Let me now assure you that every potential reader of your book has questions about and need for *faith, hope,* and *love.*

My wife and I are learning to cook together and enjoy eating good, nutritious food at home instead of processed, prepared food. Certain "seasonings" seem to bring out the best taste in all kinds of food—citrus juices, pepper, and the greatest of all of these—salt. As you cook the seeds in your bag and prepare the entrée of your book, season all your chapter dishes with these:

Faith – Write truthfully so as to build the faith and trust of your reader in you and in Christ. Life and death rest in the power of the pen, to paraphrase another proverb.[5] Pray that your seed words will make a deposit in the minds and hearts of your readers and that a harvest of faith in Christ will be produced.

Hope – I helped two business consultants write a book. Their expertise was in helping businesses minimize waste and increase profitability through change. When asked about what a consultant really sells, I expected the traditional answers—expertise, knowledge, wisdom, practical solutions to problems, etc. An answer they offered really surprised me, "We sell hope."

Hope should be the light shining through all the good, bad, and ugly you write about. I wrote a few bestselling series of books, one of which was about a 20th century faith healer and evangelist name Smith Wigglesworth. That three-book series on faith, prayer, and healing sold more than 250,000 books worldwide. Hope oozed out of every page of those pocket-sized devotionals. Write your book "that they [your readers] may set their hope in God."[6]

Love – St. Paul wrote that the only thing that matters and that the whole law is summed up in love.[7] Jesus pointed out that the two greatest commandments were about love—sincerely and wholeheartedly loving God and others as we love ourselves.[8] The seed of love sown in your book's seed-words will bring a huge harvest in God's kingdom.

Get a Bag!

In this whole chapter, I have been writing about sowing what's in your bag.

You can't give what you don't have.
You can't sow what you don't know.

I have been writing books since the late '70s. What I started writing with was spiral notebooks, yellow pads, journals, pens, pencils, markers, and papers. I also had a typewriter (even upgraded to an IBM Selectric), some wonderful secretaries, cassette tapes with recorders for dictating, mimeograph machines, spirit duplicators (ditto machines), transparencies with erasable markers and overhead projects, and slides with projectors and screens. Sounds like the dark ages of technology, aye?

Today, you and I have so many more bags within which to store the seed. Yes, the bags include smart phones, Internet clouds, computer files, digital recording, streaming video, scanning, photos, *et certera, et certera*. Your books contain the written, edited, produced, and published digital renditions of your collected seed from all those bags. Develop a discipline for saving and storing your seed. Your bags of seed can be sown into the rich soil of readers' hearts. They can bear a bountiful harvest as I have discovered not just in scores of bestselling books, but in millions of lives impacted for Christ. This proven pointer for a bestselling book is simply:

"Sow What's in Your Bag!"

3 Proven, Profitable Pointers for Marketing and Selling You &
Your Message

1. Sow what's in your bag.
2. Write to impact lives for Christ.
3. Be a disciplined writer who writes all the time.

What do you need to strategize for and implement in order to effec-
tively act upon these pointers?

_____

_____

_____

_____

-2-

GO WHERE YOU HAVE FAVOR

During the 1980s, I served as an associate pastor in two different churches with primary responsibilities in Christian education and youth ministry. Some friends of mine in youth ministry from various backgrounds gathered together under the leadership of Abingdon Press to begin writing *The Complete Youth Ministry Handbook* and *Catching the Rainbow* to provide youth teaching materials and curriculum for teenagers in various denominations and nondenominational churches. Synods, networks, dioceses, judicatories, parachurch, and regional gatherings of youth pastors and leaders began having workshops and retreats to equip one another for reaching youth for Christ.

As a contributor to these books and youth workers' training events, I began building relationships with church and lay leaders ministering to youth. A team of five of us would travel two to three weekends a month holding youth ministry workshops for Protestants, Orthodox, and Catholic youth leaders throughout the nation. It was hard work.

Often flying in small, private planes to Christian retreat and camping centers, we left at the end of each week, started the workshops on Friday evenings, and closed out with dinner on Saturday nights. Most weekends, all of us had to be back in our home churches and parishes on Sunday mornings to teach, help lead worship, preach, and hold youth meetings on Sunday evenings.

Our hard work paid off, not only in equipping youth leaders to reach teenagers for Christ, but also in building relationships throughout the country in "Serendipity" and "Catching the Rainbow" workshops. After a few years of traveling the nation, we had built an interdenominational network of youth ministry leaders who were hungry for all types of youth ministry programs and discipleship materials. One of the leaders, J. David Stone, and I were particularly concerned about what all of the counseling, coaching, and mentoring of youth pastors and lay workers had to do with teenagers relating to all kinds of issues—family problems, making right moral decisions, building healthy friendships, addressing moral issues, drugs, alcohol, and spiritual ignorance. When they had problems to solve or decisions to make, most teens would turn to their peers for counsel, not their parents, youth workers, pastors, or teachers.

What Dave Stone and I discovered was that books and curriculum for youth had to meet needs and answer real-life questions in order to be effective in equipping them to solve problems and make right from wrong choices in life. So, we wrote the first book for youth and the adults working with them on *peer counseling*. In other words, we ***wrote to the market.***

Know your market—their needs and questions.
Write to the market.
Meet their needs; answer their questions.

We wrote the peer counseling training book for youth and the adults working with them including cassette tapes containing examples and peer counseling tools. In a two-cassette binder with the book inside it, we wrote, produced, and distributed, "Someone There for Me."

Having this book and teaching resource produced and published required a business plan. We had writing goals and objectives, printing and publishing deadlines, and a budget to finance production and marketing of the material. We were self-publishers long before self-publishing became the norm for many authors.

A book is more than a published, printed product—
A book is a business plan.
A book is a business card.
A book opens the door to many specific markets
for your message.
And a book is a profitable, entrepreneurial enterprise!

If a book doesn't get publicized, marketed, distributed, and sold to the markets that need it, then the message never makes it to market, the financial and time investment in the book is never paid back, and a profit is not made to lead to more books, products, services, and resources. Books that reach the market and are sold successfully change lives and make money. Dave Stone and I had to have a business plan to not only write a book, but also to produce, market, distribute, and sell our book.

A 4-Step Book Business Plan

Years later, our simple business plan would become a bestselling E-book, *Self-Publishing Your Christian Book*. (Write me at *drlarrykeefauver@gmail.com* and I will send you one for free!) Writing to market involves these four steps:

1. Getting Started
2. Writing and Editing
3. Producing and Publishing
4. Marketing, Distributing, and Selling Your Book

All of these steps take time, money, and hard work. As an author, you need to have a plan for writing and editing your book. Then you must *do it*. For years, I have been a disciplined writer getting up early five to six days a week, writing and editing four to six hours daily producing over sixty books, published in twelve languages, with over two million in sales worldwide.

Dave and I also had to find money to invest in ourselves and our book projects. This first book project later renamed, *Friend to Friend*, cost us $5000 each (which investors loaned us) to produce and publish.

Now, here are the keys to sales and becoming a bestselling book with our first book out of the chute:

1. **We identified a market profile** (Christian youth and adults leading, guiding, teaching, mentoring, and coaching them). We already had thousands of youth and youth workers that we had favor with—they knew us through our youth ministry workshops.

2. Next, **we wrote material that practically and truthfully answered their questions and met their needs.** *How do we make right choices? How do we identify our real problems and understand our real feelings? Once we know our biblical options for making right decisions, are we willing to make the right choice and then do what's necessary to live it out?*

3. Then, **we invested in ourselves.** Many authors want somebody else to invest in their book project. Listen, if you are not willing to invest in yourself—if you don't believe in yourself, how do you expect others to invest in you and believe in your message?

4. **We planned out a marketing, distribution, and sales strategy to sell our books.** Remember that you don't just sell a book, you sell an author.

The author is an experienced, equipped, and educated expert in the topic.

I had a doctorate in pastoral counseling and years of experience in youth ministry. Dave had decades of experience in Serendipity workshops and a M.R.E. (Masters Degree in Religious Education). We were marketing and selling ourselves and our message. We believed in what we wrote and the products and services we produced. They were excellent; they worked. Lives were changed by Jesus Christ through our Kingdom business. We planned out youth ministry events; mailed out flyers and sample books; sent publicity kits out to denominational youth leaders; and contacted everyone by mail who had been at our past youth training events. We asked everyone we knew to buy and use the books with youth in youth groups, support and rehab centers, family counseling centers, Sunday School classes, camping and retreat programs, etc.

5. **We went where we had favor.** For the first six months after the book's publication, we traveled around the nations speaking at and leading youth workshops, retreats, events, and seminars. We carried, shipped, and lugged around heavy boxes of books and resources, read all of them including our own, worked the book tables, reviewed and recommended books and resources, and sold all 2,000 books and cassette tape resources, not only making back our investment, paying back our investors, but also making a 100 percent return so we could write and produce more books and resources for youth ministry.

Becoming Bestselling Authors

When we went where we had favor, youth and youth workers not only bought our books for themselves, they would often buy two or more. Here's our God-given sales pitch:

"Don't be selfish.
Never just buy a book for yourself.
God has already shown you at least two other people
who need this book.
Buy three (at a discount, of course).
Give two away to answer their questions,
meet their needs, and bless them.
Tell everyone you know about this great resource."

Take your book and published messages, devotionals, curricula, novels, podcasts, streaming videos, newsletters, online courses, webinars, etc., to the world. All of this begins with reaching out to those who know you and your message. Invite them to pray, invest in you and your message, buy your books in multiple copies and by the cases, promote and even sell your book to their friends, church members, and work colleagues. All of this creates a buzz and market demand for your book.

One youth minister on our training teams in the youth ministry workshops was a bubbly, dynamic Christian named Joani. She loved our book and cassette resource. A few years after our second printing, she married another Lutheran youth minister named Thom Schultz, who published a magazine for youth workers out of his garage called *Group Magazine.* Together they started *Group Publishing* and asked for our book, now called *Friend to Friend,* to be one of their first published releases. Over the next decade, that resource became a primary equipping book for youth in peer counseling not only in churches and in counseling youth, but also in training peer counselors in public and private high schools throughout America. Over 90,000 *Friend to Friend* books were published and sold making it my first bestselling book. Today it is also available in Mandarin and Portuguese. When you go where you have favor, God can certainly multiply your investment in your own writing a hundredfold and more!

Three More Proven, Profitable Pointers for Marketing and Selling You & Your Message

   4. **Go where you have favor.**

   5. **Know your market—their needs and questions.**

   6. **Write to the market.**

What do you need to strategize for and implement in order to effectively act upon these pointers?

_____

_____

_____

-3-

Implement a Writing, Editing, Publishing, Distribution, and Sales Strategy

You can write a book if you start, run, and finish the race. Develop a writing, editing, publishing, and marketing plan. Focus...Fight...Finish. Stop thinking and praying about writing a book...just do it! Identify and put in writing your top three to five SMART goals with realistic times and dates that are specific, measurable, and aligned with your values. Make a project plan for each goal (see mine at the end of this chapter). Without a vision people perish. Write your vision/goals down! People increase retention of something by 87 percent when they write it down. Smart in my mind stands for: Stated/Specific, Measurable, Achievable/Attainable, Realistic, and Timely. Let's look at the goals needed in each aspect of your Business Strategy.

1. **Write down and implement a business plan**. Every book has a business plan. You are an entrepreneur. Creating a product,

your book, is only part of the overall strategy to market and sell you and your book. Never just sell a book. You must take your books to branding and your message to market.

- *Focus* – What is the mission, purpose, and vision of your business, ministry, and entrepreneurial enterprise. Is it your dream to be a coach, speaker, mentor, business leader, teacher, equipper, motivator, or _____? Your book is just one product among many books, products, and services to come that revolve around your story, witness, testimony, life lessons and experience, expertise, skills, knowledge, and wisdom. Write down the steps toward actualizing your dream. Find a dream coach like David Youngren, www. davidyoungen.org, who can help you define, describe, and actualize your dream(s). Many new authors have a dream just to write and publish a book. But if it doesn't reach the market and sell, then the book will have no impact on the lives of others. What results do you expect your book to have in sales in the first six months from its release, and then the first year, two years, five years, etc.? As a business card, what doors do you expect your book to open for you, your future books, products, and services? Who needs to first see your book to give you input in shaping it, writing it, endorsing it, publicizing it, and selling it? Where on the Internet will people be able to find and buy your book? How will they know about it?

Understand that outcomes have a marketing context. Focus on your market profile. Who will be reading your book and needing its answers and having their needs met by the essential and practical information in your book, products, and services?

Since your ultimate focus in life is Christ, what does He want to say and do through you to impact, change, and transform the lives of others as well as the cultural institutions that need your message?

- *Fight* – Publishing your books, message, products, and services to the world is a fight. The inner struggle in your soul will be harsh. Doubts, insecurities, fears, and anxieties will surface and seek to overwhelm you. You must see yourself as a success and winner. When fights and failures come your way, and they will, are you so committed to the message Christ has given you to publish that you will fight through to a breakthrough and not quit? When one plan within your strategy fails, will you see yourself as a failure, or will you refuse to quit?

The plans of the diligent will prosper.[9]
God gives you infinite plans and opportunities.
The only way you can fail at accomplishing God's plans is to quit.

You will have to fight through financial challenges, criticism, distractions, self-doubt, insecurities, stress, lack of time and money, and spiritual attacks. When I am coaching authors, ghostwriting or editing for them, and equipping them in making and implementing marketing and sales strategies, I have to pray for them and exhort them both to pray and enlist the prayers and intercessions of others. I remember E.M. Bounds writing, "Without prayer, nothing happens." Prayer sharpens your focus and connects you and those praying with you in agreement with God's will in heaven to be done on earth. Jesus promises, "Take this most seriously: A yes on earth is yes in heaven; a no on earth is no in heaven. What you say to one another is eternal. I mean this. When two of you agree together on anything at all on earth and make a prayer of it, my Father in heaven goes into action. And when two or three of you are together because of me, you can be sure that I'll be there."[10]

Let me assure you that the good fight of prayer is essential to the success of marketing and selling your books, products, and services. A team of intercessors on your behalf must pray without ceasing...as you must do as well. God has given you a message, vision to write down, plans, strategies, and a purpose for your book. Someone needs the very message you are penning in order for their day of salvation, deliverance, or healing to come. Don't give up. Fight!

- *Finish* – St. Paul wrote that he had fought the good fight, finished the race, and kept the faith (2 Timothy 4:7). Yes, he had to focus, fight, and finish. You have to finish your book. I have worked with scores of authors over the years who worked hard to finish writing their book only to fail to publish it. Or, they printed and published their book, but never marketed, distributed, and sold it. I have had countless calls from authors saying, "Dr. Larry, I have boxes of my books sitting in my garage (basement or storage unit). Can you help me get them sold?" They had failed to fully implement a business plan for writing, editing, producing, printing, publishing, marketing, distributing, and selling their books.

Bestselling Authors Finish Strong

For over forty years, I have been a bestselling author. I am passionate about selling my books on radio, television, airplanes, in churches, workshops, conferences, seminars, and online. At Lovejoy Church in Buffalo, N.Y., a man came up to me after I had spoken and taught there for the fourth time covering subjects on the Holy Spirit, marriage, family, parenting, the Presence-Driven life, and healing.

"The first time you preached here, you really offended me," he said getting right in my face.

Backing away, I responded, "Forgive me. That wasn't my intent. How did I offend you?"

"You took ten minutes out of your preaching time to talk about and sell your books," he continued.

"And how did that offend you?"

"I felt you were arrogant, proud of your stuff, and out to make a buck."

I paused a moment because his facial expression suddenly changed, and a smile began to form on his face. So, I ventured a question, "Well, did you buy any of my books?"

"Just one," he confided.

"And how did that work for you?'

Before I knew it, he was hugging me and crying, "It saved my marriage. I've bought and read four more books of yours. Our family relationships have wonderfully improved. We so thank God for you."

Three of the books he had bought and shared with his family were the three titles in my bestselling *Lord I Wish* series. As of the writing of this book, the publisher has reported that *Lord I Wish My Husband Would Pray with Me, Lord I Wish My Family Would Get Saved,* and *Lord I Wish My Teenager Would Talk with Me* have sold over 45,000 books in the U.S. In the first decade of this century, GoodTV in Taipei, Taiwan, published all three titles in Mandarin. Only God knows to date how many tens of thousands of those books have gone out throughout the Chinese-speaking world. In Canada, *100 Huntley Street* put together a weeklong campaign for family salvation. They used the family salvation book and spent an entire week with me broadcasting to the nation sharing how to witness to family members and to pray for family salvation. We sent out thousands of books and received tens of thousands of prayer requests. A year later, a report showed how thousands of testimonies had poured into the studio from family members who received Jesus Christ as Lord and Savior. With no apology and in full confidence and boldness, I would go anywhere, publish, preach, and teach the messages God has given me in order to cross the ultimate finish line for selling a book—the salvation, healing, or deliverance of a soul redeemed by the risen Christ.

Becoming a bestselling author is hard work. You must plan the work of marketing and selling, and then work the plan. Remember you are writing to be read not to become rich. The purpose of becoming a bestselling author is never about making lots of money from book sales; it's about reaching thousands of readers with a message from Christ that will save, redeem, restore, renew, transform, meet their needs, and bring healing to their hurts. Og Mandino in *The Greatest Salesman in the World* wrote, "I am here for a purpose and that purpose is to grow into a mountain, not to shrink to a grain of sand. Henceforth I will apply ALL my efforts to become the highest mountain of all and I will strain my potential until it cries for mercy."[11] I hear the message of focus, fight, and finish in his words; do you? More importantly, will you just do it?

It's about making an impact, equipping and empower people to change, and ultimately equipping the saints for the work of service that God has for them in their families, churches, businesses, and communities.

Are you willing to implement a complete business strategy to focus, fight, and finish strong in publishing the message(s) God has given others through you?

Three More Proven, Profitable Pointers for Marketing and Selling You & Your Message

7. Write down a business plan that includes effective strategies for marketing and selling you and your book.
8. Implement your plan.
9. Focus, fight, and finish. Don't quit.

What do you need to strategize for and implement in order to effectively act upon these pointers?

_____

_____

_____

_____

_____

-4-

NEVER WALK ALONE—BUILD A TEAM

The enemy of your soul hates you, your message, books, products, services, and desire to become a bestselling author. Why? He simply doesn't want the good news of Christ to be published. Authors always seem surprised that I know the lies the enemy whispers in their ears about how impossible writing, publishing, and selling a book is. Since I have heard the enemy's lies for decades, and he never creates anything new, then I know the same old fiery darts he has flung toward myself and other authors will be shot their way as well. Have you ever heard one or more of these when planning to write a book?

1. *You don't have enough money.*
2. *You don't have enough time.*
3. *You don't have enough smarts to write down anything good and worthwhile.*
4. *You don't have anybody to help you; you're all alone.*

5. *Even if you do write and publish it, it'll never sell or make a difference.*

God gave me a vision to equip the saints for the work of the ministry in the early 1990s. Our family had just left a successful career in ministry in a mainline denomination rapidly losing faith and members. Leaving that denomination left us broke, jobless, and directionless. God spoke to me, "Build a faith ministry." A what? "Write books, speak, preach, and teach, and equip the saints," He went on to say.

I felt all alone. Yes, I had a few men in a Bible study group who were supporting us for a time financially and in prayer. Yes, my family was fully intact and for one another. But all those ministry colleagues abandoned me and publically ridiculed and criticized my decision to walk away from my denominational membership and credentials after being twenty-two years on their team. In fact, the president of the denomination, fearing my resignation might split the church, rushed to the scene and did damage control. We met briefly so he could say to me, "You know that leaving the church means your career if finished. You'll never preach or pastor again. You might as well sell insurance."

In spite of the enemy's attacks and lies, we discovered then the truth of the cliché, "What doesn't kill you makes you stronger." The promise of the Scriptures was affirmed in the words of the song, "You'll Never Walk Alone." Christ promises to be with us always even until the end. God never leaves nor forsakes us. Our source isn't our job or work; God is our Source.

Over the coming years, I would discover that no writer or author ever pens a book and then publishes it without the amazing grace and help of God and others. Becoming a bestselling author takes a team.

The writing and editing team. The first books I "wrote for hire" for a publisher were the Smith Wigglesworth series. I went to meet with a publisher named Tom Freiling at Creation House. I had at least a dozen of my own book ideas and titles to pitch to him. I was already a accomplished ghostwriter working with Gospel Light and Henrietta Mears' material, *What the Bible Is All About,* writing for Josh McDowell (*The Father Connection* and *Truth Matters*), as well as with Gary Smalley (*Making Love Last Forever* curriculum). I thought I was a "all that and a bag of chips." Tom wasn't impressed, nor was he interested in my book ideas.

Tom informed me that if I really wanted to become a successful author, I needed to write books that the market wanted and needed. I should write something that would sell, in other words. Publishers create a market for certain types of books that will sell. It's called the publishing business. If you don't publish books that sell and make money, then you go out of business. It's as simple as that.

"Smith Wigglesworth is really hot," Tom confided. You need to write books using his material. We need something right away to capture the market trends toward classic Pentecostal types like Wigglesworth, Kuhlman, Maria Woodworth-Etter, and John Lake. We need material about Azusa street as well."

Tom was talking in a foreign language to me; I knew nothing about these people. I had left a mainline, liberal denomination who thought these holy rollers were kooks. I was Ivy-League educated and clinically trained with a doctorate in ministry. So, writing flakey material based on some faith healers was nowhere on my radar.

"If you are willing to write the books we need that will sell, then I might consider publishing some of your books," Tom pitched to me.

"I'm game," I warily responded.

"Okay, we'll book you a flight out in January to go to the Assembly of God Archives in Springfield, Missouri," Tom instructed.

"Oh, does Wigglesworth work there? Will I be able to interview him and read some of his books?"

Tom paused. Then he laughed. "Smith Wigglesworth was a healing evangelist who died in the late '40s. He never wrote a book and was an illiterate plumber most of his life. Didn't learn how to read until later in his life. Never read any book other than the Bible. Yet, he became a world-famous healing evangelist. People are really interested in his teachings on prayer, faith, and healing. He's hot right now. We've got to publish something soon to capture the market."

Tom went on with his plan, "So, you'll fly out to Springfield. Your expenses will be paid. Get a motel close to the Archives. You can research all the notes that people took from hearing him preach and teach. You can also read the letters he wrote to people. And you can read the newspaper clippings and magazine articles written about him and his crusades. Then come back to me with a plan for books that will sell about him and his message."

Long story...short. I did just that. I returned back to Creation House with three devotional booklet ideas titled, *Smith Wigglesworth on Prayer, Smith Wigglesworth on Faith,* and *Smith Wigglesworth on Healing.* These pocket-sized, thirty-day devotionals were published, marketed, and the three together sold over 126,000 books. Then Creation House asked me to write devotionals based on those other Pentecostal faith healers and those eight books in the *Charisma Classics* and the *Charisma Classics Lessons Series* sold over 80,000 books.

I discovered from that experience it takes a team to write, edit, produce, publish, market, and sell books. The wonderful people God brought into my life in the early years at Group Publishing, and later at Creation House, taught me how to become a better writer, and then how to ghostwrite and edit the writing of other authors. It's a humbling experience to have experienced editors mark up and redline one's manuscript. It's also awesome to see how they make not only your writing but also your book produce, read, look, and feel really professional and excellent. Such excellence really honors God.

In recent years, my joy has been to pass it forward in writing, editing, and coaching new and upcoming Christian authors as they move into their journey of becoming bestselling authors in their spheres of influence and beyond. The team begins with investors, authors, and editors and moves into a Production Team.

The Production Team. Time and space doesn't permit me more than an overview here of the production team an author needs. Some authors simply use a publisher program on their computer and then go to a local printer or Fedex-Kinko's shop to publish their book. However, a professional self-publisher like Xulon Press, has a whole team that designs covers, typesets the interior text file of a book, creates digital files for E-books, Kindle, Nook, etc., registers the ISBN number, proofs and corrects the print files, and uploads the files to the "print on demand" (POD) presses or offset presses for large volume (usually 1000+) print runs.

These professional production teams save an author time and money and also produce a trade-level, classy looking book that can be proudly displayed on a bookstore shelf or in an online bookstore like Amazon.

The Marketing, Distribution, and Sales Team. You need a team of people to get your book in Amazon's bookstore as well as other online bookstores. Distributors like Ingram, Anchor, and Appalachian can put your books into bookstores and fulfill orders for your books from individuals, bookstores, organizations, and businesses. You also need to have a sales and distribution plan for selling your books, products, services, coaching, events, online courses, and webinars, etc. There are online marketing and selling platforms that can take your message to market by helping you build a following through social media and the Internet. People can coach you, train you, and integrate into your website or develop for you a new online site for publishing you and your message globally.

I am devoting much of my time to coaching authors in the whole process of marketing and selling themselves and their messages. I have had teams of people help me in the past take my message to market and my books to branding. Now, I have the joy of doing that with other authors.

The Personal Support Team. For me, that began with my parents and siblings in my growing up years. They believed in me and the calling on my life. Then I met God's greatest gift beyond Christ...my wife. Without her support and love, my confidence would really be in the tank. Over the years, prayer and accountability partners, professional colleagues, Christian leaders in business and the church, and scores of Christian friends around the planet have undergirded me, encouraged and prayed for me, and given me wise counsel. Confidence is rooted in an attitude of gratitude for God's love in Christ, His power in the Spirit, my family, friends, and colleagues in the church. And there are so many Christian leaders and Kingdom business people who have invested time and money in me to bring provision to the vision God has given me.

Confidence sells books. I had the privilege of working with Dr. Keith Johnson in the writing and editing of his book, *The Confidence Solution.* I learn so much from the authors with whom I coach, write, and edit. The enemy of your soul will try to erode or rob you of your God-given confidence. Becoming a bestselling author requires

confidence. Keith and I read what some others had to say about confidence...

Leadership expert and best-selling author John Maxwell is continually asked about the greatest qualities a leader must possess. He asserts that the leader's greatest asset is confidence. "Confidence in oneself is the cornerstone of leadership. It is difficult for those who do not believe in themselves to have much faith in anyone else. Self-confidence brings confidence in others."

Meg Whitman, who in seven years grew eBay from zero to 50 million customers and into a multi-billion-dollar global corporation, said this of her leadership priorities before stepping down as CEO to run for governor of California: "Hire the right person for the right job at the right time and who has the right values. I cannot stress this enough. Reorganize early and often. Transform change and uncertainty into opportunity."

Darren Hardy, Success magazine publisher and editorial director, said, "Whether leading a nation, a multi-billion-dollar corporation, a small sales team, or a family, the qualities of a leader are the same. A leader instills confidence and helps people become more than they are. Leaders illuminate the path for others to journey forward, farther than they thought possible by themselves."

Who can argue the business wisdom of the man who founded the dominant retail chain in the United States—Wal-Mart. Sam Walton said, "Outstanding leaders go out of their way to boost the self-esteem of their personnel. If people believe in themselves, it's amazing what they can accomplish."[12]

I like the way Keith defined confidence: "Confidence is a positive belief in yourself, your potential, and your abilities. Confidence produces a feeling of certainty and hope empowering you to perform at your best, create workable solutions to your problems, think big about your future, take calculated risks, and act effectively to achieve extraordinary, outrageous results, and success for you and others."[13]

The Scriptures tell us that our confidence is in the Lord, and that we should not throw away our confidence (Proverbs 3:26; Hebrews 10:35). My becoming an author and then reaching a dream of becoming a bestselling author, an international speaker and teacher, along with desiring to be America's Best Author Coach, begins for me with confidence. God gave me a vision and dream as a child to take the message of the gospel to the nations. I had no idea how that would happen, but I believed that anything was possible with God. He was my confidence.

He put the desire in my heart to go to an Ivy-League school and to earn my doctorate by the time I was twenty-five. I really wanted to help Christian people with discovering the power of loving relationships—loving God, others, and themselves. So, my D.Min. and post-doctoral clinical training was in pastoral counseling particularly in marriage and family. Christ instilled confidence in me to start writing in my late twenties, become the senior pastor of a large church in my thirties, and become the executive pastor of a megachurch in my forties. He also inspired me to write a bestselling book by the age of thirty-five and numerous bestsellers thereafter—fifteen bestselling books and book series in all. None of those desires and dreams would have been possible without confidence in the Lord.

Let me ask you, "In what or whom have you placed your confidence?" Without confidence in God, your dreams will be devastated and your hopes crushed. You will become discouraged and start believing the lies of the devil which I wrote about at the beginning of this chapter. Without teams of believers around you, your ability to write, produce, publish, market, and sell you and your message will never happen.

Are you believing the truth about who you are in Christ as an author?

Are you recruiting teams all along the way to help you?

> *Now this is the confidence we have in Him,*
> *that if we ask anything according to His will,*
> *He hears us.*
> *And we know if He hears us, whatever we ask,*
> *We know that we have the petitions that we have asked of Him.*
> (2 John 1:14-15)

Three More Proven, Profitable Pointers for Marketing and Selling You & Your Message

10. Reject and rebuke the lies of the enemy.
11. Recruit teams to help you.
12. Be confident in the Lord and the vision/dream He has given you.

What do you need to strategize for and implement in order to effectively act upon these pointers?

_____

_____

_____

_____

_____

-5-

RELATIONSHIPS ARE EVERYTHING— NETWORK WITH OTHERS & CREATE A FOLLOWING

When creating a marketing and sales plan for you and your message, imagination two powerful images—a tsunami and a tornado. Your message is buried under a mountain of more than 1.4 million new books published globally and 328,000 published nationally each year. Your rollout and book launch needs to be a tsunami creating buzz particularly online and in social media. Like a tsunami pushing away everything in its path, your book doesn't need to wipe out the New York Times Bestseller list or top the CBA bestseller list. Remember that a tsunami starts deep beneath the ocean floor with an earthquake or volcano. Its immediate effect isn't felt immediately. Nonetheless, the ocean terrain at its point of origin certainly is shaken. The energy and force moving a mountain of water pushes out a huge, unstoppable wall of water that moves forward powerfully across the ocean slamming into every shoreline in its path with life-changing, history-making impact.

Your book launch needs to build the momentum of a tsunami by starting where you are, going where you have favor, and moving out from those who know you and your message to those that share it. Referral and endorsements are essential and powerful to the beginnings of both marketing and selling your book.

Following the initial impact of your marketing tsunami, a whirlwind is spinning and creating a tornado-like tunnel into which hundreds and then thousands of people are swept becoming your emerging following and thus your market. This market is created by events, social media, and online blasts that put your name and message in front of thousands, tens of thousands, and ultimately millions of potential followers, readers, listeners, and viewers of your message.

Let's overview and chart the path of "going into all the world" with the publishing of your message and the selling of your books, products, and services.

1. **Let everyone who knows you or about you hear about your message/book's release.** The start of the tsunami is contacting every person who can give you input on your book's content and title. A title is like a website metatag. It has key words in it that online searches will be able to pick up. These words resonate with readers, listeners, and viewers who have needs and need answers for specific issues of life. Potential book buyers are facing critical questions and life issues that must have godly,

truthful answers *now*. Others have deep emotional needs and hurts which will respond to your message which can bring hope, understanding, comfort, and healing to their lives.

- Put together lists of people who can give you input and become a focus group for your book. Acknowledge them in the book.

- Prepare an overview in pdf of your book and send that out to all kinds of people—the messenger with expertise, credibility, believability, and integrity—to endorse your message/ book. Gather endorsements from big names in your circle and "no-names." From the big names, also get a commitment from them that they will help you promote and even sell your books by preaching, buying, selling, and sharing them with family, friends, work colleagues, churches, civic organizations, and every friend or follower they have on social media like Facebook, Twitter, Linkedin, and YouTube. Let the tsunami of your book's release sweep out to all those relationships you have and gather back in commitments to talk about, publicize, endorse, and give or sell your book in the first ninety days after its release.

- Some authors seek to have an Amazon bestselling book. Do this by asking everyone you know to go to the Amazon bookstore the day or week of your book's release and buy it. Ask them to request all of their family and friends to buy it. Create a tsunami of orders on Amazon. Most pundits say that selling 300 books in print or more than two thousand books in digital format like Kindle will push a book up into Amazon's top-ten bestsellers in a day. However, your marketing and sales strategy is not a one-day sales event.

- You need a marketing and sales platform online that will sell you, your message, your products, and service for the next year and even years. That platform collects names and email on landing pages that promote you and your message through free products, E-books, and newsletters. This marketing plan is a tornado sweeping continually over the Internet world. As people search for ways to meet their needs and answer their questions related to your message, they search for and find your website or landing page. As they sign in, you capture their contact information and begin marketing and selling you and your message.

- Book launches and signings at bookstores, in churches, and through special events do create a buzz especially in your first inner circle of friends, family, church members, and business colleagues. Set up a number of these in ever widening circles. Promote these events on podcasts and streaming video. Let people join you live through a Twitter periscope.

These ideas are not exhaustive but simply illustrative of beginning the marketing and sales campaign that is ongoing for you and your message.

Marketing is a sprint and a marathon—a tsunami and a tornado. Have marketing and sales campaigns and programs that continually promote you and your message for years to come. Your goal is to build a following and your own market.

2. **Network with other authors, speakers, leaders, media, and organizations.**

Broadcast and online media needs to know about you and your message through online ads, podcasts, interviews, reviews, and events like infomercials, webinars, etc. Research who is out there and what is the best way to get free media exposure, aka Trump, as well as scheduled interviews. Become an expert pundit in your field on talk shows.

I know pastors who have networked with others pastors, churches, and parachurch organizations to promote, sell, and host fellow pastor-authors in events to promote their message. At times, they build entire church campaigns and small group studies for church around their books. Take a step back. Put together a flow chart that starts with the first groups of people you want to give input, endorse, and promote your book. When you reach out to them, ask specifically for what you need from them.

For example, after I had completed writing *Lord I Wish My Family Would Get Saved,* I contacted program coordinators and hosts for Christian television and radio programs. I sent press releases and sample reviews of the book to magazines and journals. I shared the release of the book with dozens of pastors and church leaders asking them to 1) tell everyone in their networks and mailing lists about the book, and 2) consider having me teach and/or preach in their churches or conferences about family salvation. I continued to follow up with everyone I spoke with and started scheduling local congregational events and conferences throughout Brazil, Asia, and North America. Had YouTube been available to me, I would have created streaming videos. I regularly emailed all my contacts about what God was doing through the book, events, and media outreaches on family salvation. I sent out video and audio recordings of my teaching and events. Here's the bottom line:

**Network with everyone you know,
using every platform available to you on the Internet, Phones,
and Direct Mail, to offer yourself and your message
to them in every format available.**

Create the Right Publicity and Follow Up with Every Lead!

When I coach and consult with authors, churches, and ministry organizations, I help them identify who they have in their phone contacts and email/address/social media databases. We segment those lists and determine what needs and answers their book(s), programs, courses, products, and services will meet and provide. Sending the right publicity and promotional material to the right market, written in the right language to address their customer needs and demands is critical for getting a positive response. Sending out general publicity to a general audience may create 1-2 percent in leads. Reaching specific market profiles, with specific products and services that focus on important and essential questions and needs, will provide a much higher response in leads and sales results.

Putting together a team of people to help you send out this publicity and then effectively following up with all the responses is essential for achieving positive, profitable results. Plan how you will network with people and organizations and write out exactly what you want to communicate and why they need you and your message. The earlier principle I wrote about of sowing and reaping applies again here. Sow the right seed into the right soil and cultivate it. Have realistic expectations—expect a lot of rejection or disinterest, but also expect opportunities to emerge. Always follow up on every lead while focusing on meeting needs and answering questions as you confidently sell you and your message.

Relationships Are Everything

Love God and love others as you love yourself; isn't that the core of living out the Christian life? Marketing and selling you and your message isn't about getting people to buy your products and services so that you have a sustainable stream of income. Your desire is to serve your readers, viewers, listeners, and customers.

"How may I serve you?"
That's the attitude for effectively becoming a bestselling author.

The price you will pay will be hours on the phone building relationships with your readers, customers, and Christian leaders. As you build a following and a market base, you will also build meaningful and lasting relationships with people who need your expertise, message, and loving care.

In the back of almost every one of my fifteen bestselling books and series, I have listed contact information. I created an easy to find website with my contact information. People from all over the world call and email me when they have read one of my books, gone through a study guide or curriculum, or heard me in a podcast or seen me on streaming video. They want a real caring person who will listen, give them wise and godly counsel, and pray with them. Remember, your message forges a relationship with the reader/listener/viewer that communicates the love, mercy, and grace of God to others. I tell authors that when your book is transparent, authentic, and real, your reader begins to trust you and relate to your life experiences. Readers begin to see Christ living in and through you and want to know more about the God who loves them.

One of my author friends often says, "I truly believe that a book can change 10,000 lives or 1 life that changes 10,000 lives." The relationships that are formed through marketing and selling you and your message really impact lives for Christ. I developed wonderful relationships with Dr. Ron Cottle and church leaders in his Christian Life Educators Network. They invited me to speak about writing and publishing books at one of their annual meetings.

I was speaking to a group of international educators from North and South America, Europe, and Asia. Many of them used my college-level, online and DVD courses in their Bible Schools and College curricula on marriage, family, and parenting. While I was speaking, a group of about twenty people in the back were making quite a bit of noise that was distracting as they were talking with each other. Distracted, but also pushed for time, I continued to speak louder and more emphatically. As my volume increased, so did theirs.

My twenty-minute speaking time limit came. I closed my talk, and walked away from the podium as the entire conference was dismissed for a morning break. Suddenly, the noisy group from the back rushed up to me led by their excited ringleader. "I am the interpreter for this group," he explained. "Sorry for my noise but everyone in our group from the Ukraine was so thrilled when you, Dr. Larry, were introduced before your talk. All of them recognized you from your course and book on marriage which they have been studying."

I know I looked puzzled. Before I could speak, the animated, Russian interpreter went on, "You see, a few months ago our Bible school started your new course on Christian marriage with your textbook that had just arrived in Russian, 'Lord I Wish My Husband Would Prayer with Me: Tearing Down the Walls in Marriage.' Only one copy arrived, so we tore the book apart chapter by chapter and each couple got one chapter, read it, and then passed it on to another couple in the class. Already, over a dozen couples have been reading your book which is blessing them and helping their marriages heal and grow. Thank you."

I was speechless. I had not been aware that my book, already translated in Spanish, Mandarin, and Portuguese was now in Russian. God works in mysterious ways through books touching people even in faraway places. I am so grateful I had been obedient to write. I have learned that someone, somewhere in the world, is waiting on the other side of a writer's obedience to write "the book." Books can meet needs, answer questions, and change lives through God's grace, mercy, and love.

Permit me just one more story. For years our ministry had a toll-free number that rang in my office and was forwarded to my home number when the office was closed. A few years after I had discussed *Lord I Wish My Husband Would Pray With Me* on a Canadian Christian television program, my home phone rang after 11 p.m. Rarely did I receive a call so late unless it was an urgent call from family or a counseling crisis intervention call. My caller ID indicated the call was coming from Toronto. After a quick hesitation, I decided to answer the phone instead of allowing it to go to the answering machine.

A man with a heavy, Hindi accent spoke, "Good evening, is this Dr. Larry Keefauver the author and marriage counselor?"

"Yes," I cautiously replied.

"Forgive me for calling so late but my wife and I are sitting here weeping after reading your book on praying with each other," he confided.

"Okay," I responded and then just listened.

"We are both family practice physicians here in Toronto. We practice medicine in the same office. Earlier this week as we left the office and walked out through our reception area, we noticed a book lying on a chair. It was your book about husbands praying with their wives.

"Both of us are devout Hindus and know the power of prayer. So your book title intrigued us. So after dinner tonight, we started reading it together. We couldn't put it down. We prayed the prayers you suggested praying. We have had problems like every couple has in marriage. But we have stuck together. We love each other. Your book really helped us pull down the walls that have been between us through prayer."

"Thank you for sharing," I responded as he paused for a moment.

"We just accepted Jesus as our Lord and Savior in this prayer you taught us to prayer in your book. Do you have time to talk with us about that?"

Stunned and momentarily at a loss for words (imagine that!), I then spent another thirty minutes with them, sharing about being a follower of Christ and the need to find a church family in the Toronto area. Because I had networked with many Canadian churches and leaders over the years—relationships are everything, I was able to give their contact information to a local pastor in their area. Books can really impact lives for Christ!

Networking with readers and leaders, building relationships, developing a following, and serving others through loving and caring relationships is essential to becoming an impactful bestselling author, speaker, teacher, and witness for Christ. Read Philippians 2. Serve others with your books, products, and services. God will then open doors and meet your every need as a bestselling Christian author.

Three More Proven, Profitable Pointers for Marketing and Selling You & Your Message

13. **Build relationships and create a following for you and your message.**

14. **Network with other people, organizations, churches, and networks who can promote and publicize you and your message.**

15. **Relationships are everything. Build loving and caring relationships with your readers, viewers, and listeners. Serve them for they are your market!**

What do you need to strategize for and implement in order to effectively act upon these pointers?

_____

_____

-6-

Be Presence-Driven: *You're a Sailboat not a Rowboat*

When God is in the plan, the book, and the message, it will become a bestselling book in His timing and for His purpose to give Him glory. I am a Presence-Driven, bestselling author. When I discovered the power of the Holy Spirit in my Christian walk, I wanted to write about Him and share the Spirit's power, fruit, and gifts with anyone who would listen to my message.

When you are Presence-Driven, and I will share more about that with you in a moment, you are open to hear from God any message He wants to share through you. When you are in His Presence, you can hear those messages in a variety of ways—through Scripture, prayer, dreams, visions, the wise counsel of others, and even through trials and tribulations. One of my bestselling books came out of a nightmare.

In 1999, I had a nightmare in which I saw my brother at the Great White Throne judgment among the lost. His look at me across the abyss caused me to wake up suddenly in a cold sweat and trembling.

I went to my office and prayed, "Lord, why isn't my brother saved?" The Spirit responded, "What is it in you that keeps Al from being saved?"

I started writing down all the walls in me that kept my brother from Jesus and resulted in a book, *Lord I Wish My Family Would Get Saved*, published in 2000 by Creation House and still in print.

Subsequently, the book was published in Mandarin, Indonesian, and Portuguese. I traveled all over Asia, US, Canada and Brazil preaching and teaching on family salvation. At 100 Huntley Street with David Mainze, I spent one week on their programs speaking about the book. They asked their viewers and partners to send in pictures and prayer requests for family member salvations. Hundreds of thousands of requests were received which papered the walls of their chapel, studio, and common area during which staff prayed daily for salvations. Over $100,000 CAD came into the network building memorial offerings based on Acts 10 for family salvation. Tens of thousands of testimonies came in during the year of salvations. Miracle upon miracle happened.

Many churches, like LoveJoy in Buffalo, set up wailing walls with pictures and prayer letters for family members. Service after service, week after week, congregations would pray for family members to be saved and people would stand up and give testimonies about family members being saved. Some would bring their family members to church and the whole church would rejoice at their baptisms.

Throughout the nations preaching and teaching and on television as well through TBN, CTN, Cornerstone, and Daystar, I talked about the book and asked viewers and congregants alike to pray for my brother's salvation. Literally millions were reached with this message, and I believe hundreds of thousands did pray. In 2003, Pastor Henry Hinn invited me to come to his church in Vancouver and preach on family salvation. When I mentioned my brother in the message and asked people to pray for him, Henry stood up and gave a prophetic word, "Within a year, your brother will be saved as a result of heart problems."

In November of that year, a church in Spokane, WA, emailed me and Judi asking us to come on Valentine's Day weekend in 2004 to a campground in the mountains outside of Spokane to lead a marriage seminar for about twenty couples. We already had personal plans on that weekend for us to celebrate in Florida. We had no desire to travel across country to do a marriage seminar in the snow-covered mountains for a few couples. I prepared to write an email declining the request and recommending a couple in the NW who could do the retreat. Judi agreed with me. As I wrote the email the Holy Spirit prompted me, "Do the retreat. You will have a divine appointment."

Before I pushed "send" on the email to decline the invitation, I told Judi what the Spirit said. She paused and then said, "Okay, we should do it, but you had better have heard from the Holy Spirit on this!" I accepted the invitation, so on Friday, February 14, 2003, we boarded an early flight from Orlando to Denver, changed planes, and flew on to Spokane. The church's pastor picked us up at the airport, and we drove about two hours into the mountains and arrived at a snow covered campground...cold, cold, cold.

It was a good retreat. Marriages healed, divorces canceled—all miracles in and of themselves. So, Sunday afternoon, we boarded our cross country red eye flight back from Spokane to Denver for an hour layover and then we were to fly to Orlando. Judi asked on the flight, "So what was the divine appointment?" I responded with all the spiritual spin I could muster about healed marriages and cancelled divorces, but she seemed unconvinced about the critical necessity for us making such a long trip out of Florida during the winter.

When we landed in Denver, I turned on my cell phone and checked for messages. Only one voice mail was on my cell. I listened. It was my brother. I hadn't talked to him on the phone for years. We had exchanged polite emails and Christmas cards over the years. All of my efforts to reach out to him especially with Christ were rejected. He had thrown my books away and answered my emails with, "The force be with you."

Hearing his voice in the voicemail shocked me. He was weeping and I had no idea how he had gotten my cell number. I learned later he called my sister, who with the rest of my family had been praying for him to be saved for years. As a teenager, Al had been hurt by words from a church leader and walked out of church and relationship with the Lord never to return.

I listened to Al's message that was broken up with sobs. "Larry, bro, I must talk to you. My heart's broken. Where in the world are you?"

I was stunned. I was listening to this voicemail on my cell standing in the Denver Airport. My brother lived in Denver, just fifteen minutes from the airport!

I called him. We talked, and I told him I was actually in the Denver airport. He asked me to stay over and talk with him the next morning. I agreed. Judi was thrilled for the divine appointment between my brother and me. She flew on to Orlando, and I made arrangements to delay my flight and return the next evening. I stayed at a hotel next to the airport and looked forward to reuniting with my brother the next day.

What prompted his phone call to me on the day I would be in Denver? It was millions of prayers and the curious meeting of a woman through an online dating site. Months before our divine appointment, Al had met Kim online. He was divorced. She was a widow. She lived in Colorado Springs to be close to her brother's family. The week before Valentine's Day, Al told Kim he loved her and wanted to marry her after dating for months. She said no. She couldn't marry someone whose god wasn't her God. She was a committed, born again Christian. By the way, Kim's brother is the President of Focus on the Family which is why they lived in Colorado Springs. The Holy Spirit had prepared a secret weapon to reach Al's heart through a dating site—of all things!

So, that spurned proposal had broken his heart, just as the prophetic word from Pastor Hinn had promised. He had heart problems. He had been weeping and unable to go to work or even drive since that rejection.

When Al showed up at the hotel room on Monday morning, I was surprised to see an attractive blond at his side. It was Kim. He had asked her to drive him over to the hotel. The three of us sat on the floor and wept. Al told me his story about how Kim's persistent witness to him over the months hadn't gotten through to him until she said no to him. His hardened heart had been broken and now he was ready to hear from me and her about Christ. We talked. Confessions and tears flowed. Love and forgiveness from the Father and between brothers overflowed. My brother accepted Jesus as Lord and Savior on that hotel bedroom floor and all of us wept, rejoiced, prayed, and then went to breakfast at Denny's.

I had never seen in my thirty-plus years of ministry such a radical, wonderful, instant change in a person. Al was reborn right before our eyes. By the way, the following Easter, I had the privilege of baptizing Al in the Atlantic Ocean and officiate the beach wedding for Al and Kim in New Smyrna Beach, Florida. Now that's a miracle! That's Presence-Driven!

Receive Your Message and Vision from God

I can truthfully say that becoming a bestselling author is not about trying, though it is hard work—it's about trusting. God in Christ is my

BFF. The more you hang out in His Presence, the more you hear the messages He wants you to share. A good person leaves an inheritance to his/her grandchildren (Proverbs 13:22). Part of that inheritance is a legacy in print.

Being in God's presence is like being in a cloud, not just the Exodus cloud leading God's people through a wilderness, but also like being in cloud storage on the internet. Think about this. Being in the cloud of God's Presence opens you up to downloads from His word and Spirit pouring into your heart and mind filling you with wisdom, knowledge, and understanding. I have discovered that being in His Presence births Power and Passion for me, which in turn, births Purpose, Plans, Process, and Productivity for writing books, editing, doing good works that glorify Him, and most importantly, serving and loving Him, others, and myself.

For fifteen years after 1990, His Presence downloaded into my spirit, mind, and heart inspiring the writing of over forty books and curriculum series, including bestselling books about the Holy Spirit such as the notes for the *The Holy Spirit Encounter Bible,* and eight 30-Day *Holy Spirit Encounter Guides* that all told sold over 210,000 copies. After writing them, God put into my heart to write *Experiencing the Holy Spirit* and *Inviting God's Presence* which together sold over 30,000 books.

As I traveled, taught, and preached throughout India, Nepal, Indonesia, Singapore, Malaysia, and Taiwan, church leaders would ask us to equip Asian families in the areas of holy, healthy, and whole relationships. Often converted believers would bring traditional and ungodly family practices into their newly saved Christian homes. The mind of Christ is needed in one's relationship with the Father. The biblical truths for living out loving relationships in families need to be learned, understood, and practiced.

A pastor in Singapore who had his church's six hundred cell group leaders go through the *Holy Spirit Encounter Guides* knew that Judi and I had led parenting and marriage workshops in Malaysia and Indonesia. God's Presence opened a door for us to connect and discuss the important need for his young adults (over 90 percent of his church members were under the age of thirty, single, and first generation believers). While we were in Malaysia teaching in a Bible School, that pastor invited us to come to his church for a weekend and conduct a parenting seminar. He said, "Bring 2,000 of your parenting books when you come as well for our people to have."

His request had been birthed in God's Presence. We heard God's mandate to write a parenting book. The rub was that we were in Kota Kinabalu, Sabah, Malaysia for a week-long Holy Spirit conference; we would come back to Malaysia to teach at The School of Acts for a week, and then go to Singapore with our book, which had not yet been written or published, to lead a parenting seminar. Yet, when it's a God idea and not just a good idea, His Presence opens the doors to make the impossible possible.

Our Holy Spirit conference in Kota Kinabalu had night meetings, so Judi and I had the day time hours free to write. God's Spirit helped us understand that Asians didn't need to do family the way Western Christians were doing it resulting in skyrocketing divorces, teenage rebellion, and moral relativism. Family wasn't built on traditional, cultural values. All relationships were to be holy, healthy, and whole by being rooted in the foundations of biblical principles shaped and defined by absolute truth. We easily found seventy-seven biblical passages that formed the basis of a new book, *The 77 Irrefutable Truths of Parenting*. The book was written, edited, typeset, and printed in two weeks in Malaysia. It was shipped out from Kula Lumpur on a Thursday, arrived a few hours before the start of the seminar on Friday evening, and completely sold out (2,000 copies) in one hour after the seminar. I planted, Judi watered, and God gave the increase—an instant bestseller birthed in His Presence.

The rest of the story is that God also gave us three other books— *The 77 Irrefutable Truths of Marriage, The 77 Irrefutable Truths of Prayer,* and *The 77 Irrefutable Truths of Ministry*. Some of these titles have been translated into Portuguese, Indonesian, and Mandarin. I recently was contacted by a French publisher for the parenting book as well. Tens of thousands of these books in print and digital formats have saturated Asia, Brazil, and North America and been featured on our 220 Family Forum programs broadcasted by GoodTV throughout the Chinese-speaking world.

Psalm 45:1 declares, "My tongue is the pen of a ready writer." The only way that happens is when an author dwells in God's Presence and allows God's Spirit to birth the purpose for each book, the plans for writing, editing, and producing the book while overseeing the process of marketing, distribution, and sales. Then, real productivity and prosperity will be birthed for both the readers and the writers who are obedient in taking God's message to the market.

Leave a Legacy in Print

Becoming a bestselling author starts with sowing yourself, your message, and your book into the lives of those people who know you—friends, family, church, business, community, and social networks like social media. Every family member should write a book leaving a legacy in print for that family...a memoir, if you will, of that family's spiritual and genealogical journey. We are to leave our grandchildren not just a physical inheritance, but also a relational and spiritual inheritance as well. I call these legacy books which are filled with testimonies and witnesses to God's saving, healing, and delivering power in Christ Jesus.

Pastors often preach a "home run" series of messages at least once each year that should be transcribed, flowed into a book, formatted, edited, and published not only for the present congregants but also for new converts and members coming into the church in the future. With the ease and accessibility of self-publishing tools, pastors can easily plan a writing and preaching schedule which will produce a book a year. Their churches can help them develop a marketing, distribution, and sales plan for these books which not only equips and blesses the church members, but also provides members books to give to those outside the church to help heal hurts and meet needs. Books become tremendous ministry and evangelism tools in the hands of believers.

Christian business leaders need to write books about their Kingdom business mindset, business principles, and company's DNA for employees and customers. Books are training and equipping tools to define a company's brand and put forth the company's mission, vision, purpose, and ethos. I have so enjoyed coaching CEOs, educators, business leaders in all professions, scientists, health care professionals, and self-help motivators and speakers in writing books that provide wonderful equipping tools for Christians in every walk of life. If you are a business leader, write a book, learn how to market and sell you and your message in the marketplace.

Can you imagine a sailboat only functioning as a rowboat? Believers are designed as sailboats which are powered by the wind of His Spirit to go where Christ leads us. So often, we act more like rowboats never raising the sails He has given us to catch the wind of His Presence. We row hard, try hard, and rely completely on our own talents, skills, strength, and efforts to move forward. I know that authors often try so hard to catch the attention of publishers, the media, buyers, and customers. They are working hard at rowing in the writing, editing, publishing, and marketing of their book that they lose sight of the Bestselling Author of the Bestselling Book of all time. The Holy Spirit is the eternal ghostwriter of history's bestselling book, the Bible.

Be still and know God. Stop rowing so hard. Raise the sails of your meditation, prayers, Bible reading and study, giving, serving, loving, evangelizing, and all the spiritual disciplines. Catch the wind of His Spirit. Dwell in His Presence. The more you are in the Presence of the bestselling author of all time and eternity, the more you will be changed in His Presence and become like Him. So, as a bestselling Christian author, I can say to you what Paul writes in 1 Corinthians 11:1, "Follow my example as I follow Christ."

Three More Proven, Profitable Pointers for Marketing and Selling You & Your Message

16. **Receive God's message for your book as you dwell in His Presence.**

17. **Be open to God ideas for your books that can come to you through wise counsel, dreams, visions, Scripture, life experiences, and His still, small voice in your spirit.**

18. **Become a Presence-Driven author who is the pen in the hand of eternity's Bestselling Author.**

What do you need to strategize for and implement in order to effectively act upon these pointers?

_____

_____

_____

-7-

BECOME AN EXPERT—BE TRANSPARENT & TRUTHFUL

One of my most successful bestselling books with almost 130,000 in sales is *Hugs for Grandparents* published by Simon and Schuster. Every grandparent needs hugs. I learned that from my parents who always had me hug their parents every time we saw them. I have learned that from my adult children who have taught our seven grandchildren to hug us whenever we see them. Yeah, it's sort of awkward for our teenage grandsons to give us a big hug, but you know what, it feels so good when a hug happens.

Years ago, I heard a pastoral counselor speak at a retreat for teenagers, parents, and youth workers. He said that every teenager needs at least ten hugs a day. After the session, we went to lunch in the camp's dining hall. I arrived late and ended up at the back of the line with a few of the other adult youth workers. It seemed like it was taking forever for the line to move forward. Usually the food line went really fast as all the teenagers rushed through the line, loaded their plates with the food they liked, and rushed to a table to sit with their friends. So, a slow food line at youth camp was an anomaly.

After about fifteen minutes of the line going nowhere, I impatiently marched up to the front of the line where the food trays were stacked. There I saw the problem. A fourteen-year old guy was hugging each person in line and then handing the next person a food tray. I impatiently asked him, "What are you doing?"

"Just catching up," he smiled as he hugged me and gave me a tray.

Hugs for Grandparents was a God idea, but thankfully it wasn't just a good idea. There is a huge need and thus a massive market for hugs. The publisher asked me to write it for them. It was a gift book that zoomed off the charts into bestselling status. What made it so appealing? The book was filled with personal stories reminiscing about wonderful, scary, and poignant moments I had shared with my own grandparents. The book was real, truthful, transparent, and filled with laughter and tears.

An expert marketer once told me that ***every sale is an emotional buy***. A buyer's emotions are engaged and triggered by the look of the book's cover, the title, a word or image. The potential reader/buyer immediately responds to a need that book's message can meet.

I share with authors that the first impression marketing tools a book has are:

- The title and subtitle
- The author's bio on the back cover

- The back-cover copy with endorsements
- The Table of Contents
- The Introduction, Foreword, or Preface

Bestselling books make a good first impression.

The first things a reader sees about a book hook an emotion, build mystery or curiosity, promise to reveal a secret, or provide a key that will unlock skills, healing, health, wholeness, or meaning and purpose. The chapter title may be questions that the reader is personally asking and hoping to find answers to. The right chapter title can be the whole reason a reader buys the book. That chapter for him/her can give an answer, solution, skill, or key desperately needed.

In the digital world of marketing and selling you, your message, or your books, products, and services— key words that name your book or your brand help people find you, your website, books, product, or service. Facebook, Twitter, and LinkedIn are primary digital outlets. Every word counts. Words like bestselling, author, publishing, marketing, selling, profitable, proven, and pointers helped readers like you find me and this book.

Why is the author's brief bio and end of book, *About the Author*, so important, along with those endorsements? People want to hear from someone who's an experienced, educated expert. I can't tell you how many doors my earned doctorate has opened for me in speaking, teaching, selling books, and consulting with church and business organizations.

Endorsements establish your credibility and trustworthiness. Readers also want to know that other experts and people just like them have benefited from you and your message. The endorsements that don't fit on the back cover of the book can be put in their entirety on the first pages inside the cover of a book.

To Be a Bestselling Author, Become an Expert

People want to be informed, imparted to, and impacted by people who have experienced, practiced, and walked out the truth of their message. Imagine me writing a book about becoming a bestselling author and never have written a bestselling book. What a scam that would be. Judi would often remind me through the years, that being an educated expert in counseling and pastoral psychology wasn't enough for people to want my books or be in our seminars. I had to walk the talk and share the truth about my everyday life and relationships. Truthfulness and transparency were essential for people believing the message.

Being an expert in biblical studies was important to me as a writer. I learned Greek and Hebrew as an undergraduate. Understanding how to have loving relationships was critical to me as a pastor who would be counseling and teaching believers. So I worked hard not just in academic studies for theology, exegesis, and church history, but also devoured the training I received in psychology, counseling, and ministry/serving skills. Yet, academic credentials weren't enough to equip me to write bestselling books. I needed years of experience filled with struggles, trials, problems, marriage and parenting successes and failures, in order to validate the truths of God's messages written through me in books.

In the 1990s, I discovered a way to become an expert in writing about subjects I knew nothing about. It was called ghostwriting. Experts in health, medicine, nutrition, science, history, and business as well as in ministry and theology started asking me to help them write their books. They gave me journals, slides, handwritten notes, recordings, videos, diaries, articles they had written and written about them, as well as typed pages, manuscripts, and computer files filled with content. Often they would say to me, "Here's my message, find and write the book." A preventative medicine physician, Dr. Reginald Cherry, asked me to write his first book, *The Doctor and the Word,* and then his next one, *The Bible Cure.* I had to study, research, and learn all about nutrition, fitness, and health based on biblical wisdom and truths. Under his tutelage, I became an "expert" in the field. I also learned from him and his organization how to develop a following using direct mail, television, newsletters, and developing supplement products for helping his patients and ministry partners. By the way, those two books have sold almost 420,000 copies.

Then God inspired another idea in this field of expertise. Another Christian physician, Dr. Don Colbert, wanted to write a series of booklets about preventing and curing illnesses like heart disease, cancer, diabetes, obesity, etc. These books about health, nutrition, and wellness became *The Bible Cure Booklets*. I helped to write and edited the first twelve booklets in the series which sold over 2.44 million books worldwide. I later helped write and edit another nine health, wellness, and nutrition booklets for a Christian chiropractor. I also learned that when you know what is right and don't do it, it's sin (James 4:17). Judi and I both learned what a killer obesity can be. Over a period of about two years, we acted upon the truths we learned from these doctors, and under a doctor's supervision, each of us lost over sixty pounds and started living a healthy lifestyle with good nutrition, fitness, rest, and sufficient hydration. Authors must walk their talk in order to be credible experts for their readers.

People will buy and read books from experienced, truthful, experts who really want to educate and equip people for living a full and abundant life in Christ—body, soul, and spirit.

Lately, I have been ghostwriting and editing books for Christian psychiatrists. It's been amazing to learn from them how much I need to change and grow in my soul and family relationships. I have become a learner for life as well as being married for life and a parent for life. At times, despite book sales, becoming a bestselling author is serving as an expert who leaves a legacy in print and becomes a bestselling author.

All of us are experts in our own life's story and what God has done in, through, and around us to save, heal, and deliver us. That's why your first book may well be a memoir, witness, or testimony book that shares with others your personal story and how God in Christ by the power of His Spirit helped you become an overcoming victor, not a victim in life. You can share your story about how God moved you from failure to success, from losing to winning, and from success to significance.

If you are not an expert in something, become one if you want to take your book to branding and your message to market.

Get equipped, earn a degree or advanced degree in a field of study where your expertise can help others. Become trained and certified in a specialty and then start writing about it.

Remember, you are not writing textbooks. I am working with a number of authors who are taking their dissertations and theses and converting them into books that are readable and practical for a non-academic market. Define the market profile of your readers and write books to answer their questions and meet their needs or heal their hurts. Write at a reading level that they can understand your words and message. You are not writing to impress people; rather, you are writing to impact them for Christ. Again, bestselling authors are able to truthfully say to their followers, viewers, listeners, and readers, "Follow my example as I follow Christ."

Three More Proven, Profitable Pointers for Marketing and Selling You & Your Message

19. Become an expert.
20. Be truthful and transparent.
21. Walk your talk; live what you write.

What do you need to strategize for and implement in order to effectively act upon these pointers?

_____

_____

_____

_____

_____

FINAL WORD

Be Encouraged!

Why are many of the traditional publishing methods becoming obsolete? Too often the publishers viewed the authors as the market instead of creating markets for the authors' messages. Yes, you have to make money to stay in business, but publishing is more that an ego trip for authors or a profitable business for publishers. Publishing empowers authors to take their message to market and transforms their books to branding.

You will never become a published writer or bestselling author until you start. Getting started in writing, or producing, or marketing and selling your book is simply taking the first step. If you want encouragement, email me at lkeefauv@christianpublishing.com or drlarrykeefauver@gmail.com. I can help point you in the right direction and share with you a free book, *Self-Publishing Your Christian Book*.

All the authors I coach, edit, or write for, I pray for. We are mandated by the Scriptures to pray for one another and encourage one another. My prayer is that this book has been an encouragement to you. Furthermore, I want to do one more thing before you set this book down, I want you to pray about what you just read. Thank you for the privilege of sharing my message with you in this book. I hope I have the privilege of connecting with you on Facebook or Twitter in the future as well.

Lord Jesus Christ, Son of God,
Have mercy on this author,
May _____ become the pen of a ready writer in Your hand.
Grant _____ all that is needed to walk out the dream, vision, purpose,
and calling you have on _____'s life.
Fill the sails of _____'s life with the wind of Your Presence.
In the name of the Father, the Son, and the Holy Ghost.
Amen.

Postscript

21 Proven, Profitable Pointers for Marketing and Selling You & Your Message

1. Sow what's in your bag.
2. Write to impact lives for Christ.
3. Be a disciplined writer who writes all the time.
4. Go where you have favor.
5. Know your market—their needs and questions.
6. Write to market.
7. Write down a business plan that includes effective strategies for marketing and selling you and your book.
8. Implement your plan.
9. Focus, fight, and finish. Don't quit.
10. Reject and rebuke the lies of the enemy.
11. Recruit teams to help you.

12. BE CONFIDENT IN THE LORD AND THE VISION/DREAM HE HAS GIVEN YOU.

13. BUILD RELATIONSHIPS AND CREATE A FOLLOWING FOR YOU AND YOUR MESSAGE.

14. NETWORK WITH OTHER PEOPLE, ORGANIZATIONS, CHURCHES, AND NETWORKS WHO CAN PROMOTE AND PUBLICIZE YOU AND YOUR MESSAGE.

15. RELATIONSHIPS ARE EVERYTHING. BUILD LOVING AND CARING RELATIONSHIPS WITH YOUR READERS, VIEWERS, AND LISTENERS. SERVE THEM FOR THEY ARE YOUR MARKET!

16. RECEIVE GOD'S MESSAGE FOR YOUR BOOK AS YOU DWELL IN HIS PRESENCE.

17. BE OPEN TO GOD IDEAS FOR YOUR BOOKS THAT CAN COME TO YOU THROUGH WISE COUNSEL, DREAMS, VISIONS, SCRIPTURE, LIFE EXPERIENCES, AND HIS STILL, SMALL VOICE IN YOUR SPIRIT.

18. BECOME A PRESENCE-DRIVEN AUTHOR WHO IS THE PEN IN THE HAND OF ETERNITY'S BESTSELLING AUTHOR.

19. BECOME AN EXPERT.

20. BE TRUTHFUL AND TRANSPARENT.

21. WALK YOUR TALK; LIVE WHAT YOU WRITE.

About the Author

Larry Keefauver with his wife, Judi, RN, have been in ministry for over 40 years. Both have extensive experience in counseling and mentoring. Their three adult children are married, actively living for the Lord, and are parenting seven grandchildren. Judi and Larry have traveled internationally leading seminars and conferences on family, marriage, parenting, church leadership, and spiritual growth. They have an international TV program, Family Forum, seen throughout Taiwan, China, Korea and on the Internet through GoodTV.

Dr. Larry Keefauver is professionally and educationally trained in pastoral counseling. He holds degrees from the University of Pennsylvania and Texas Christian University. His wife Judi is a registered nurse. Bestselling family books include: *Lord I Wish My Family Would Get Saved, The 77 Irrefutable Truths of Parenting* (with Judi), *Proactive Parenting—The Early Years, The 77 Irrefutable Truths of Marriage* (with Judi), *Lord I Wish My Teenage Would Talk With Me,* and *Lord I Wish My Husband Would Pray with Me.* Judi's devotional book for women is *Be.*

With over 2.5 million books worldwide in 11 languages, Dr. Keefauver is the noted author of *Inviting God's Presence, When God Doesn't Heal Now, Experiencing the Holy Spirit, The 77 Irrefutable Truths of Ministry, Hugs for Grandparents, Hugs for Heroes, Commanding Angels—Invoking the Standing Orders, From the Oval Office: Prayers of the Presidents, The 77 Irrefutable Truths of Prayer* and *Friend to Friend.* He edited the bestselling *Through the Bible* in one-year curriculum— *What the Bible is All About* (Gospel Light). Other Lifeway Press adult curriculum includes *Making Love Last Forever* (with Gary Smalley), *Truth Matters* (with Josh McDowell), and *The Seasons of a Man's Life* (Patrick Morley).

He has written extensively for Christian magazines and is a contributing editor and writer for *Ministry Today, Kairos,* and *Harvest Times,* is a member of the International Coalition of Apostles and the Open Bible Faith Fellowship, and is involved in financial, business, and church consulting. He and Judi have bases in Orlando, Florida, and Central Texas.

Dr. Keefauver is also senior ministry partner and board member with Eagles' Wings Ministries where he gives apostolic oversight to pastors, churches, and non-profits throughout the US. And he is Senior Editor for Xulon Press, a division of Salem Communications where he coaches, edits, and mentors authors in implementing marketing and sales strategies. For more, go to: www.xulonpress.com or www.christianpublishing.com

Larry and Judi are members of the St. Nektarios Orthodox Mission in Waxahachie, Texas.

Want to know more about Dr. Larry Keefauver? Google his name... search his name on Amazon.com to see many of his books and resources... go to www.doctorlarry.org. Other sites for information: www.bookgrowschurch.com, www.ymcs.org.

Also, watch these videos:

How to Birth Your Book

http://xulonpressblog.com/birthing-your-book

Xulon Press Editing Services

http://xulonpressblog.com/xulon-press-editing-services

Contact Dr. Larry at: lkeefauv@christianpublishing.com or drlarrykeefauver@gmail.com.

Facebook: Larry Keefauver

Skype: Larry.Keefauver

Twitter: @lkeefauv

Linkedin: Larry Keefauver

www.doctorlarry.org

Discover Dr. Larry's bestselling books on Amazon...

Hugs for Grandparents

Experiencing the Holy Spirit

When God Doesn't Heal Now

Lord I Wish My Husband Would Pray with Me

Lord I Wish My Family Would Get Saved

Lord I Wish My Teenager Would Talk with Me

The Holy Spirit Encounter Guides (8 vols.)

The Holy Spirit Encounter Bible

Smith Wigglesworth on Prayer

Smith Wigglesworth on Faith

Smith Wigglesworth on Healing

The 77 Irrefutable Truths of Prayer

The 77 Irrefutable Truths of Parenting

The 77 Irrefutable Truths of Marriage

What the Bible is All About 101, 102, 201, 202

Friend to Friend

Friends and Faith

Starting a Youth Ministry

...and many more...

Appendix 1

Be Presence-Driven

So here's what being a Presence-Driven author becoming a bestselling author looks like:

The Presence-Driven Life

EXODUS 33:12-16

Be Filled with the Spirit

"And do not be drunk with wine, in which is dissipation; but be filled with the Spirit." (Eph. 5:18 NKJV)

Hoist Your Sails & Stop Rowing

PANIYM–Presence

The person

The face

The presence

Before God face to face

Presence Brings Perspective & Vision—Isa. 43:18-19

God's Presence births – Genesis 1

Presence ⇨(births) Power & Passion

Isa. 37:32b; Acts 1:3; Gal. 2:20-21

Acts 1:4-8

Romans 15:13

Power ⇨ Purpose

Eccl. 3:1-8

Isa. 14:25-27; 46:11

John 12:27

Rom. 8:28, Eph. 1:7-14

Purpose ⇨ Plans

Jer. 29:11

Ps. 33:10-12

Prov. 16:9, 19:21, 21:5

Isa. 30:1, Acts 5:38-39

Plans ⇨ Process

Romans 5:1-5

2 Peter 1:5-9

Process ⇨ Productivity & Prosperity

Ps. 144:12-13

Matt. 13:23

John 12:24-26; Jn. 15:8

Rom. 5:3-4; Gal. 2:20f

Presence-Driven Life

Presence ⇨ Purpose; Purpose ⇨ Power;

Power ⇨ Plans; Plans ⇨ Process & Practicing the Presence;

Process ⇨ Productivity & Prosperity

Matt. 25:14ff

Want to know more about the Presence-Driven Life and the Presence-Driven Church?

Email: drlarrykeefauver@gmail.com to receive an entire list of available resources in .pdf and mp3 formats.

Appendix 2

COLLECTING ENDORSEMENTS

I mentioned how important endorsements are for you to accumulate for you, your message, materials, events, etc. Here are some examples I received over the years. Also, you can go to Amazon.com and look at many of my book covers or back covers and see how endorsements can be used in there.

ENDORSEMENTS FROM LEADERS

I've traveled extensively with Dr. Larry Keefauver and have been present with him in countless engagements including one-one interviews, mass meetings, private settings, television and radio interviews. He is a gifted communicator, and a man of integrity and principle. Dr. Keefauver is passionate in his beliefs, yet expresses himself with dignity and professionalism. I highly recommend this man as one to listen to.

Dr. Tom Gill

Director, TLR Ministries

As Executive Director of the Covenant Marriage Movement I would like to offer my endorsement to Dr. Larry Keefauver as one who articulately communicates his heart, and the heart of those he serves, with regard to whatever subject matter is introduced. He is a man of character and of steadfast love for the Lord.

In His Service,

Phil & Cindy Waugh

Executive Directors, Covenant Marriage Movement

www.covenantmarriage.com

I have heard Larry Keefauver speak in formal and informal settings and he is amazing. He is not your typical religious expositor. His profound understanding of society and human nature is refreshing. He can mix humor with sober truth in such a way that commands attention without being overbearing and judgmental. He is a good friend. You will greatly enjoy his presence.

Alan Babcock

Sr. Pastor, Greenville Christian Life Center

www.greenvillechristianlifecenter.com

Larry Keefauver is a voice to our nation. Larry represents so many segments of the body of Christ. He is well received in churches of all denominations and is well loved by Christians of every race. He is articulate, informative, engaging and sure in his presentations. He has spoken for us on several occasions. We have a 3,000 member church and he is well loved and appreciated by the people here in Jacksonville, Florida. His books are on the shelves of many great leaders across this nation. Larry Keefauver speaks for me.

Bishop Vaughn McLaughlin, *Presiding Bishop of Covenant*
Fellowship International
Pastor of the Potter's House Christian Fellowship, Jacksonville, Florida

I am pleased to recommend Mr. Larry Keefauver as a capable and qualified spokesman for your program. He has appeared on WACX TV in Orlando many times and he will be an asset to your program.

Claud Bowers
President, WACX TV

Dr. Larry Keefauver has spoken a few times at Eagle's Nest Christian Fellowship in San Antonio, Texas, a congregation of approximately 3,000. Not only is he very knowledgeable on his subject matter, but he has a great delivery of the word. He is sensitive to the Holy Spirit's guidance as he teaches and brings life to his audience.

Respectfully,
Pastor Rick Godwin, Eagle's Nest Christian Fellowship
14015 San Pedro Avenue, San Antonio, Texas 78232
Tel. No. 210-402-0565

Over the years I have known Larry Keefauver I have been impressed by his passion for families and marriages, as well as his integrity in all that he does. His extensive study and travel gives his vision for families and marriages depth and insight.

Rev. Ted Bichsel

Pastor of Care Counseling Marriage and Family

Smithtown Gospel Tabernacle

Insight leads one forth into victory! Larry Keefauver is man of insight, discretion, and wisdom. Not only, does he have great understanding of God's Word and how it applies to the world around him, he knows how to communicate these principles to others! Without knowledge and vision a people can perish...Larry, releases both to those who are willing to listen!

Chuck D. Pierce

President, Glory of Zion International, Inc.

Vice President, Global Harvest Ministries

P. O. Box 1601

Denton, TX 76202

940-382-1166

I have known Reverend Dr. Larry Keefauver for the last 10 years and he is a highly respected ordained minister, journalist, author, communicator, and licensed counselor. His work among churches and non-profit humanitarian organizations in Southeast Asia has been nothing short of outstanding. I am proud to be a friend of Dr. Keefauver and highly recommend him as a Church commentator and analyst in the Christian world today.

> **Reverend Dr. Kong Hee**
> *Senior Pastor*
> *City Harvest Church (Singapore)*

Dr. Larry Keefauver is a very powerful conference and seminar speaker, and author, who is noted for his in-depth understanding in Church history, Church government, and the proper structure of the Church, and knows very well the true meaning of "separation of Church and State."

He is well versed in the subject of marriage, family, and youth counseling. His gifting in the area of family relations has enabled men and women in the USA and many other nations to grasp a greater understanding of their union in holy matrimony, and how to maintain a healthy and supportive relationship in their marriage. Tens of thousands of marriages have been strengthened by the teachings in his books, and through his seminars and conferences.

Dr. Keefauver has established Christian schools and assisted in starting Christian Universities in the USA and other countries. He has appeared on several television shows, as well as conducting his own ministry program.

Dr. Keefauver's accomplishments speak very highly of his skill and ability to speak on the behalf of the Christian Community and the Christian Church. I could think of no one else more qualified to represent Christianity, or to lead us in a national prayer for the upcoming presidential election.

Much more could be said, but I appreciate the opportunity to speak briefly on behalf of my family and the ministry of Harvest Time International in recommending Dr. Keefauver.

Pastor A. Johnson Murphy Jr.
Harvest Time International

Like Esther of old, the ministry of Dr. Larry Keefauver is for "such a time as this." His education, experience and commitment to pray and capacity to get others to pray has prepared him, as no other, to lead the nation in "Campaign 44." Dr. Keefauver takes serious the biblical mandate "to pray for kings and those in authority." But equally important is his unique gift of getting others to do so as well. Indeed he is God's man to mobilize America to pray for the coming election.

Rev. Dr. James M. Hutchens
Chaplain (Brigadier General) US Army (Ret.)
President & Chairman of the Board, Christians for Israel (USA)
www.c4iusa.org
Editor, The Jerusalem Connection
Tel: 703-707-0041
Fax: 703-757-6501

To Whom It May Concern:

I am pleased to endorse Dr. Larry Keefauver as one of the most outstanding teachers and writers in the US Church today. His keen insights and wise observations are extraordinary. As an avid Larry King watcher and fan, I hope that our friend Larry Keefauver will be invited to appear. His message is relevant and clear; his presence is appealing and persuasive; his knowledge of the issues of the upcoming election is profound.

Sincerely,

Ronald E. Cottle, Ph. D., Ed. D.
President, Beacon University
Columbus, Georgia

Larry Keefauver is a gifted speaker, minister, writer and **editor.** He is **versatile and insightful as he shares with** great passion concerning family values being restored in our nation. Larry is a man of prayer and he will be a great encouragement to all who hear him speak.

—Naomi Dowdy, Trinity Christian Centre, Singapore

"At a time when our nation is facing an election that provides the voter with a serious choice, Dr. Keefauver in a non-sectarian and non-partisan manner encourages the general audience to not only be sure to register so that their personal opinion can be included in the ballot totals but to also pray that the outcome God desires will happen."

—Stephen Strang
Strang Communications
Publisher of *Charisma, Ministries Today, New Man, Christian Retailing* and *Spirit-Led Woman* magazines

Praise for INVITING GOD'S PRESENCE

"If I were writing a manual for how to enter the presence of God, this would be my textbook."
—Tommy Tenney, CEO/president of GodChasers.network and author of *The God Chasers*

"In this creative new book, Dr. Keefauver gives us incredible steps to enhance our relationship with God. If you're interested in growing spiritually, this book will share with you ways of finding God's love in a powerful and wonderful way."
—Dr. Robert A. Schuller, Crystal Cathedral Ministries

"The message of INVITING GOD'S PRESENCE is a life-changing invitation for every believer to come and dwell in His presence. We can no longer live for momentary touches from God. This book will become a way of life for those who are hungry and thirsty for more of God."
—Pastor Sam Hinn, The Gathering Place Worship Center

"Dr. Larry Keefauver's passion for God and people comes through strong and clear in INVITING GOD'S PRESENCE. Sadly, all too many Christians feel that

God is distant. Instead of fellowshipping with the 'friend who sticks closer than a brother,' they struggle with feelings of unworthiness, fear, and rejection. Dr. Keefauver exposes the often invisible barriers that hinder people from experiencing God. This teaching will help believers allow God's presence to permeate every aspect of life."
—Peter Youngren, Niagara Christian Center

"FINDING GOD'S PRESENCE is fresh, insightful, applicable material on the timeless subject of inti macy with the Father. Larry Keefauver has written a practical, interactive, step-by-step manual for drawing near to God in your daily walk. This is a resource for every believer seeking to grow in a personal, life-giving relationship with God."
—Ted Haggard, New Life Church

"Dr. Keefauver has not only found the living, resident presence of God for himself but is able to communicate that presence to others. I highly recommend the reading of this book." —Dr. Fuchsia T. Pickett

"Larry Keefauver is one who will never be satisfied living on a plateau. He knows there are always new heights to conquer, and he knows you want to conquer them, too.

INVITING GOD'S PRESENCE will open the way for you to experience God's full destiny for your life."
—C. Peter Wagner, chancellor, Wagner Leadership Institute

"In these days of anxiety, fear, uncertainty, and terror, the need for the assurance of God's presence is an imperative. Larry has released a timely and much needed book that will positively impact the lives of every reader. This one's a classic."
—Dr. Myles Munroe, BFMI, Nassau, Bahamas

WARNER FAITH AUTHORS NAMED FINALISTS FOR CHRISTIANITY TODAY BOOK AWARDS

Two Warner Faith Authors have been named finalists in the prestigious Annual Christianity Today Book Awards.

- Deborah Bedford's WHEN YOU BELIEVE nominated in the Fiction Category
- Larry Keefauver's INVITING GOD'S PRESENCE nominated in the Spirituality Category

Categories include: Fiction, History/Biography, Theology/Ethics, Spirituality, Christian Living, Biblical Studies, Christianity & Culture, Apologetics/Evangelism, The Church/Pastoral Leadership, Missions/Global Affairs.

The awards are chosen by leaders in a variety of disciplines-including academia, the church, and journalism. The winners in each category will be announced in the June issue of Christianity Today Magazine.

EVANGELICAL CHRISTIAN PUBLISHERS ASSOCIATION
4816 South Ash Avenue, Suite 101
Tempe, AZ 85282
Phone: (480) 966-3998
Fax: (480) 966-1944
ECPA Web Site: www.ecpa.org

BEST BOOKS AUTHORS
PUBLISHERS WEEKLY

 # When God Doesn't Heal Now

Larry Keefauver, Author *Thomas Nelson Publishers $13.98 (192p)*
ISBN 978-0- 7852-6975-5

This honest, mature message affirms God's healing role while challenging the enduring myths many evangelical Christians harbor about healing. A myth, says Keefauver, usually has a kernel of truth from Scripture and personal experience but "is rooted in the experience of some and then masquerades as truth for all." One myth is that people are healed by their own faith. "Your healing doesn't depend on your faith," Keefauver tells readers, "but on the One in whom you place your faith." He also challenges the myths that healing requires being touched by the right evangelist or preacher or that the perfect kind of prayer can move God into performing a healing. One of the book's most passionate chapters explores the basic theodicy question: Why would a loving God permit pain and suffering? Keefauver refutes the notion that disease is a punishment for sin (one of his congregants thought that her breast and cervical cancers were God's punishment for her teenage pregnancy and abortion decades before). The book contains some powerful stories of miraculous healings but also profiles those who come home from revivals dejected, ill and doubting God. Why does God heal some now and not others? Keefauver's title reflects his view that the ultimate healing is eternal salvation, not cure from physical disease, and that those who grow closer to God during their illnesses are also, in the eternal scheme of things, victorious. (Feb.)

DETAILS

Reviewed on: 02/14/2000 Release date: 02/01/2000

ENDNOTES

1 Mark 4:3

2 Psalm 19:14

3 2 Corinthians 3:18

4 Proverbs 23:7

5 Proverbs 18:21

6 Psalm 78:7

7 See 1 Corinthians 13, Galatians 5, and Romans 13.

8 Matthew 22:38f

9 Prov. 21:5

10 Matt. 18:18-20 MSG

11 http://addicted2success.com/quotes/17-og-mandino-quotes-to-move-inspire-you/

12 Johnson, Keith Lee. The Confidence Solution: Reinvent Yourself, Explode Your Business, Skyrocket Your Income (Tarcher Master Mind Editions) (pp. 4-6). Penguin Publishing Group. Kindle Edition.

13 Johnson, Keith Lee. The Confidence Solution: Reinvent Yourself, Explode Your Business, Skyrocket Your Income (Tarcher Master Mind Editions) (p. 6). Penguin Publishing Group. Kindle Edition.

CPSIA information can be obtained
at www.ICGtesting.com
Printed in the USA
FFOW01n0926140417
34483FF